Neal Starkman, Ph.D.

connecting in your classroom

> *18 Teachers Tell How They Foster the Relationships*
> *That Lead to Student Success*

Search **INSTITUTE** | *Practical research benefiting children and youth*

To Aunt Gloria, still my favorite teacher

Connecting in Your Classroom

18 Teachers Tell How They Foster the
Relationships That Lead to Student Success

Neal Starkman, Ph.D.
Copyright © 2006 by Search Institute

10 9 8 7 6 5 4 3 2
Printed on acid-free paper in the United States of America .

Search Institute
615 First Avenue Northeast, Suite 125
Minneapolis, MN 55413
www.search-institute.org
612-376-8955 • 800-888-7828

CREDITS
EDITORS: Ruth Taswell, Kay Hong,
          Marcie DiPietro Rouman
BOOK DESIGN: Cathy Spengler Design
PRODUCTION COORDINATOR: Mary Ellen Buscher

LIBRARY OF CONGRESS CATALOGING-IN-PUBLICATION DATA
Starkman, Neal.
  Connecting in your classroom : 18 teachers tell how they foster the relationships that lead to student success / Neal Starkman.
      p. cm.
  ISBN 1-57482-858-4 (pbk. : alk. paper)
  1. Effective teaching.
  2. Teacher-student relationships.
  3. Adolescent psychology.
  I. Title.
LB1025.3.S733 2006
371.102'3—dc22

                          2005028435

ISBN-13: 978-1-57482-858-0
ISBN-10: 1-57482-858-4

ABOUT SEARCH INSTITUTE
Search Institute is an independent, nonprofit, nonsectarian organization whose mission is to provide leadership, knowledge, and resources to promote healthy children, youth, and communities. The institute collaborates with others to promote long-term organizational and cultural change that supports its mission. For a free information packet, call 800-888-7828.

ABOUT THE AUTHOR
Neal Starkman, Ph.D., has developed programs in drug education, HIV/AIDS prevention, violence prevention, and peer helping. He has written a number of books for Search Institute, including *Great Places to Learn: How Asset-Building Schools Help Students Succeed* (1999), *Ideas That Cook: Activities for Asset Builders in School Communities* (2001), and *Hey, Coach! Positive Differences You Can Make for Young People in Sports* (2004). Starkman holds a Ph.D. in social psychology.

contents

introduction **great teachers**   v

trusting teachers   1

Trusting teachers empathize with their students, give their students responsibilities, challenge them, and give up control.

engaging teachers   29

Engaging teachers make the curriculum interesting; relate it to students' lives; involve students' peers, family, and community; and allow students to be themselves.

asset-building teachers   59

Asset-building teachers incorporate Developmental Assets into the school curriculum, into the school environment, and into the community environment.

caring teachers   83

Caring teachers nurture, value, and believe in students.

hardworking teachers   103

Hardworking teachers build connections with students, throughout the school, and throughout the community.

teachers unite!   123

list of great teachers   129

acknowledgments   132

introduction great teachers

Which do *you* remember more from school—class work or teachers? assignments or friendships? tests or feelings of safety and support (or fear and discomfort)? When you have a good relationship with a teacher—or other adult at school—you feel better and you do better.

The things that matter are found between the lines, outside the books, and beneath the surface. The things that matter are found in what the teachers in this book do every day of the year.

Here, you'll meet some great teachers—teachers you'll probably wish you had when you were going to school. (Who knows? Maybe some of them *were* your teachers when you were going to school.) Not only do these teachers know their content areas, not only do they communicate knowledge and skills in an exemplary fashion, but these teachers also make their students—*all* their students—feel special. These are teachers who consider their students as thinking, feeling, growing, complex individuals with simple needs: to be listened to, respected, appreciated, trusted, encouraged, and loved. These needs may be simple, but they're evidently not easily met; otherwise, the teachers in this book would be the rule and not the exception.

What can be learned from these teachers? After all, they're vastly different from each other. They come from different backgrounds, entered the teaching profession for different reasons, work with different ages and socioeconomic classes of students from all over the country, belong to different-sized schools, and have different styles, both in the classroom and out. But despite their differences, these educators have a lot in common.

All these teachers possess five qualities that make them paragons of their field. Each of these qualities is described below. More in-depth examples appear throughout the rest of the book.

1. All these teachers are **trusting**. They seek to empathize as much as possible with their students so that they can assess the students' strengths. They believe that assigning responsibilities to their students—at whatever age—is a good thing, and they challenge students to reach or exceed their potential. These teachers don't have a strong need to control everything that goes on in their classrooms; they'd prefer that their students take over when they're ready.

2. All these teachers are **engaging**. They motivate their students to learn. They vary their pedagogy so that everyone, regardless of learning style, is involved. These teachers engage their students in a number of ways, but they regularly relate the curriculum to students' lives—inside and outside the classroom. These teachers' students want to come to class every day.

3. All these teachers are **asset building**. All of them incorporate Developmental Assets into their approach and into their curriculum. They provide an asset-rich environment in which their students thrive—in the classroom and throughout the entire school community. Their intentional focus on the assets results in a pervasively positive culture that the students participate in and make their own.

4. All these teachers are **caring**. This was emphasized—and evinced—more than any other quality by every teacher in this book. These teachers care what happens to each and every one of their students. They build relationships, they become involved in their students' lives, and they never take students for granted. They nurture them, value them, and believe in them.

5. All these teachers are **hardworking**. They spend virtually every minute building relationships with their students, providing supportive environments, and establishing liaisons with students' families and the greater community—to say nothing of ordering supplies, filling out report cards, and writing grant applications. And some of these teachers are doing all that in addition to

attending extracurricular activities, coordinating after-school projects, chaperoning field trips, coaching sports, and facilitating discussion groups.

So: Great teachers are Trusting, Engaging, Asset building, Caring, and Hardworking; that is, they *TEACH*.

Learning about each of these teachers can help other teachers accomplish two very important goals. One goal is to identify and adapt strategies that build Developmental Assets as well as meet academic objectives. (For more information on Developmental Assets, see page ix.) These strategies range from having first-grade students read aloud to their peers (Peggy Allen does that) to helping fifth-grade students start and run their own store (Kathi Swanson does that) to organizing a senior-facilitated orientation for incoming first-year high school students (Mark Hendrix does that).

The other goal is more subtle. It has more to do with personality than with curriculum, more to do with relationships than with homework, and more to do with environment than with testing. You can help your students thrive by building and maintaining strong relationships with each of them and by providing an environment in your classroom, in your school, and in your greater community that gives young people an opportunity to reach their highest potential.

the teachers in this book

Some of the teachers interviewed for this book say that since becoming aware of the importance of Developmental Assets and focusing on building them, they've spent more time trying to connect with students. They invariably note that that time is well worth it, because it connects *them* with why they became teachers in the first place: to have a positive impact on young people.

Other teachers say that since becoming aware of the importance of assets and focusing on building them, they've actually *saved* time, because they're disciplining less, they're micromanaging less, and they're "lecturing" less. They've discovered that their students revel in responsibility and that teaching has become a collection of partnerships between them and their students.

The group you fall into will depend on your style of teaching, the nature of your students, and the interaction between you, them, and your school community. One thing is certain, though: The teachers in this book will tell you that the rewards from doing what they do are immeasurable. So as you read about what each of these teachers has accomplished, think: "Can I do this? Do I want to do this? *Should* I do this?" Whatever you do, you'll do it in your own way, but I hope this book will offer you some new ideas you haven't thought of before.

The teachers in this book have been recommended to Search Institute by their principals, their colleagues, their students, and their students' families. Some of them have won awards for their achievements, but at least as many have toiled in relative anonymity. They've embraced the concept of Developmental Assets and strive to build those assets with their students. In doing so, they've found ways to make huge positive impacts on the young people they come into contact with every day. You would be fortunate to sit in these teachers' classrooms.

a primer on developmental assets

Some of the 18 teachers profiled build Developmental Assets more explicitly than others, but they all see the value in integrating them. You can think of Developmental Assets as the "essential nutrients" young people need to grow up healthy, responsible, and caring. These essential nutrients have also been found to be associated with student achievement—academic success and avoidance of problem behaviors, such as using drugs and violence. The results of Search Institute's examination of the scientific literature as well as surveying more than a million students currently point to 40 such assets.

The more of these assets that students report having, the higher their grade point average—not only for the current year, but for up to

40 developmental assets for youth ages 12 to 18*

CATEGORY	ASSET NAME AND DEFINITION
external assets	

support	1. **Family support**—Family life provides high levels of love and support.
	2. **Positive family communication**—Young person and her or his parent(s) communicate positively, and young person is willing to seek advice and counsel from parent(s).
	3. **Other adult relationships**—Young person receives support from three or more nonparent adults.
	4. **Caring neighborhood**—Young person experiences caring neighbors.
	5. **Caring school climate**—School provides a caring, encouraging environment.
	6. **Parent involvement in schooling**—Parent(s) are actively involved in helping young person succeed in school.
empowerment	7. **Community values youth**—Young person perceives that adults in the community value youth.
	8. **Youth as resources**—Young people are given useful roles in the community.
	9. **Service to others**—Young person serves in the community one hour or more per week.
	10. **Safety**—Young person feels safe at home, at school, and in the neighborhood.
boundaries & expectations	11. **Family boundaries**—Family has clear rules and consequences, and monitors the young person's whereabouts.
	12. **School boundaries**—School provides clear rules and consequences.
	13. **Neighborhood boundaries**—Neighbors take responsibility for monitoring young people's behavior.
	14. **Adult role models**—Parent(s) and other adults model positive, responsible behavior.
	15. **Positive peer influence**—Young person's best friends model responsible behavior.
	16. **High expectations**—Both parent(s) and teachers encourage the young person to do well.
constructive use of time	17. **Creative activities**—Young person spends three or more hours per week in lessons or practice in music, theater, or other arts.
	18. **Youth programs**—Young person spends three or more hours per week in sports, clubs, or organizations at school and/or in the community.
	19. **Religious community**—Young person spends one or more hours per week in activities in a religious institution.
	20. **Time at home**—Young person is out with friends "with nothing special to do" two or fewer nights per week.

continued on next page

40 developmental assets for youth ages 12 to 18* *continued*

CATEGORY	ASSET NAME AND DEFINITION
internal assets	
commitment to learning	21. **Achievement motivation**—Young person is motivated to do well in school.
	22. **School engagement**—Young person is actively engaged in learning.
	23. **Homework**—Young person reports doing at least one hour of homework every school day.
	24. **Bonding to school**—Young person cares about her or his school.
	25. **Reading for pleasure**—Young person reads for pleasure three or more hours per week.
positive values	26. **Caring**—Young person places high value on helping other people.
	27. **Equality and social justice**—Young person places high value on promoting equality and reducing hunger and poverty.
	28. **Integrity**—Young person acts on convictions and stands up for her or his beliefs.
	29. **Honesty**—Young person "tells the truth even when it is not easy."
	30. **Responsibility**—Young person accepts and takes personal responsibility.
	31. **Restraint**—Young person believes it is important not to be sexually active or to use alcohol or other drugs.
social competencies	32. **Planning and decision making**—Young person knows how to plan ahead and make choices.
	33. **Interpersonal competence**—Young person has empathy, sensitivity, and friendship skills.
	34. **Cultural competence**—Young person has knowledge of and comfort with people of different cultural/racial/ethnic backgrounds.
	35. **Resistance skills**—Young person can resist negative peer pressure and dangerous situations.
	36. **Peaceful conflict resolution**—Young person seeks to resolve conflict nonviolently.
positive identity	37. **Personal power**—Young person feels he or she has control over "things that happen to me."
	38. **Self-esteem**—Young person reports having a high self-esteem.
	39. **Sense of purpose**—Young person reports that "my life has a purpose."
	40. **Positive view of personal future**—Young person is optimistic about her or his personal future.

three years later.[1] This correlation holds true for students from all ethnic and socioeconomic backgrounds. As a matter of fact, the number of assets that students report having turns out to be *twice as important* in predicting achievement as demographic factors such as gender, family composition, socioeconomic status, or race/ethnicity. (You can read more about this research on Search Institute's Web site: www.search-institute.org.)

While certain of the assets are more predictive of students' academic achievement than others, teachers can have a tremendous influence on building *all* the assets. Here are some brief examples:

> **Other Adult Relationships** Help students identify adults in the school community who are willing to support them.
> **Service to Others** Set up a tutoring service for younger students.
> **Adult Role Models** Let students know what good things adults in school have done for their community.
> **Positive Peer Influence** Facilitate a discussion about what students can do when their friends aren't being responsible.
> **Creative Activities** Incorporate music and theater into the curriculum.
> **Youth Programs** Find, download, and pass on information from Web sites about after-school activities in the community.
> **Achievement Motivation** Set high academic standards particular to each student.
> **School Engagement** Bring students to a science museum.
> **Bonding to School** Organize a project to paint the gymnasium or music room.
> **Reading for Pleasure** Ask students to give reports on books that have been made into movies.
> **Restraint** Point out to students how much money tobacco companies make from selling cigarettes to teenagers.

[1] Scales, Peter C., & Roehlkepartain, Eugene C. (2003). Boosting student achievement: New research on the power of developmental assets. *Search Institute Insights & Evidence, 1*(1), 1–10.

> **Resistance Skills** Teach students ways to use self-control in high-pressure situations.
> **Peaceful Conflict Resolution** Ask students to recreate and role-play situations that typically cause conflicts for them.

Teachers around the country are using their own methods and incorporating others' for building Developmental Assets in their classrooms and in their communities. You'll read about some of these methods in this book—and likely you'll find yourself inspired to make even more of a difference in the lives of your own students.

None of these teachers could sustain what they do if it weren't for one other common quality they all share. It's hard to define precisely, but every teacher in this book has it. It's *passion*. These teachers have drive, an ambition to do well by their students, whatever it takes.

They *want* to come to work in the morning, they *want* to meet with their students and parents, they *want* to intentionally build assets. In short, these teachers love teaching.

For them, teaching is a challenge with great rewards, and most of them wouldn't trade it for any other profession. The passion may be there at the outset, or a teacher may grow into it. One thing is for sure: The passion that sustains, *propels* these men and women to do great work flows through them and into the students they teach.

The teachers in this book exemplify what it means to be trusting, engaging, asset building, caring, and hardworking. There are countless other ways that *you* can show these qualities. The overall goal is to help students be academically, socially, and emotionally successful. Building Developmental Assets is an effective way to achieve that goal. And great teachers are the ones to do it.

trusting teachers

> *Kids are people, too.*
>
> **KATHI SWANSON**

trust takes on many forms in teaching. At its most basic, it's giving students responsibility because you know they'll benefit from the experience, no matter what the outcome. The four teachers presented in this section are varied in their backgrounds, in their approaches, and in the circumstances of their school communities. Michael Walsh, Susie Edwards, and Kathi Swanson teach in communities that present serious socioeconomic challenges; Susan Cressey does not. Kathi and Susan knew from a very early age that they wanted to become teachers; Michael and Susie became teachers in part because they struggled in school. Michael and Susan facilitate formal asset-building programs in their schools; Susie and Kathi do not.

But all four teachers share at least one thing: the ability and desire to trust their students. Each of these teachers builds assets for and with their *students by forming relationships; and at the core of those relationships is trust.*

As you read about these four teachers, think about how they not only place trust in their students but also show that trust—because it's important for students to know that they're trusted and that they've been given responsibility. Think about the ways you place trust in your students and how you show that trust. Ask yourself: "Can I empathize with students? Can I give them more responsibilities? Can I continue to challenge them? Can I give up more control? Can I find other ways to trust?"

> > >

trusting teachers empathize with students. What in your background predisposes you to trust or not trust others, particularly students? When you were a student, were you trusted? Somewhere along the way, you've no doubt discovered that empathizing is a necessary first step to establishing a trusting relationship with anyone. When you can understand a person's behavior, take into account the person's background and history—their strengths, pressures, experiences, hopes, and temptations—it's a lot easier to gauge the level of trust to place in that person. The trust isn't blind; it's based on what you know. Teachers who can empathize with their students have more confidence in placing trust in those students.

michael walsh

> **GRADES 5 AND 6**
> **URSA MAJOR ELEMENTARY SCHOOL, FORT RICHARDSON, AK**

Some people know from the outset that they're going to grow up to be teachers. They set their sights on education. They go straight to college and get their teaching credentials, and immediately afterward they begin teaching in a school.

Other people find their calling by a different route.

Although his father and many of his relatives are educators, Michael didn't initially have a drive to become an educator himself—in fact, he *hated* school. He had little desire to learn, to excel academically, or to pay attention; he was paddled often. In seventh grade, his father—the principal of the elementary school across the street—had him come over to the elementary school to teach children with Down's syndrome to swim. It was Michael's first teaching experience. When he was 18, he began a series of alternative careers—ocean lifeguard, whitewater kayak guide, ski shop manager. Only a friend's (a retired teacher) sitting him down and forcing him to apply to college furthered his formal education.

Astonishingly, Michael claims that he hardly read a book until he was 28. When he completed graduate school at the ripe old age of 31, he and a friend went to Alaska to climb and to get jobs as mountain or river guides. He ended up managing a private airstrip in the Alaska Range. At the age of 35, he met the woman who would become his wife. They decided to settle down in Alaska, and Michael began looking for substitute-teaching jobs, principally in special education—something, at least, with which he had experience. That first summer of marriage (his seventh summer in Alaska), he worked with the "On Target" program for emotionally disturbed children. That fall, Michael landed his current job at Ursa Major Elementary School, in Fort Richardson, Alaska, an army base.

Ironically, this checkered educational background gave Michael the tools to empathize with his students. He *hadn't* been a great student. He *hadn't* liked school. He *hadn't* grasped for school curriculum knowledge. So when Michael sees young people ill-prepared for "Life After School," he understands them. And understanding them paves the way to establish a trusting relationship.

In 1999, Michael attended a training in which students from Alaska's remote bush communities talked about the importance of Developmental Assets in their lives. The concept attracted him, and he thought about how he could begin building assets in his own community. He concluded: "I'm going to keep it simple. The only way that this is going to be successful is if it's going to be self-motivating." He came up with a logo and began recruiting "asset ambassadors."

Michael asked teachers to choose students who could help out before and after school, who would welcome visitors and give tours during the day. Ursa Major now has asset ambassadors from the fifth and sixth grades. Michael also has the goal of student asset ambassadors training parents to be adult asset ambassadors.

Think of that: Fifth- and sixth-grade students are welcoming visitors; fifth- and sixth-grade students are training adults. Some schools wouldn't give students such responsibility. Some adults would say that 9-, 10-, and 11-year-olds are not sufficiently mature to be tour guides or trainers. But

Michael, along with Principal Meg Marman and others, trusts that with proper guidance, these students will do just fine. And so they do.

Each month, Michael and his students choose a Developmental Asset to focus on and build throughout the school community. They furnish an "asset wall" with the names of the asset ambassadors and news about assets. In his classroom, Michael talks about goal setting, family influences, and drugs. He reinforces the positive decisions students are making daily and illustrates how all decisions, good or bad, have import for the future. If, for example, a student is choosing not to use self-control in school, then Michael points out that that student might not use self-control when confronted with a decision whether or not to smoke or drink.

In short, Michael places trust in students on an individual level; it's a basic pedagogical shift that most teachers who teach social skills effectively know plenty about. They know that in order for students to use the skills—for showing restraint, for resisting peer pressure, for resolving conflicts peacefully—the students need to do much more than memorize the steps. They have to take the responsibility to *own* the skills, to adapt them to their own situations, and to be motivated to use them in the appropriate circumstances.

It's the same with any knowledge and skills: By placing trust in students' abilities and by giving them the tools to use those abilities, Michael helps build assets such as Responsibility, Planning and Decision Making, Resistance Skills, and Personal Power. He recruits students to spread the word about assets, and he continually emphasizes to all his students the significance of their decisions.

These teaching methods depend, though, on Michael empathizing with his students, on his understanding of their lives. That's why he puts a priority on making the assets real for students. He asks them, "How many of you think you'd be able to work a job, a real job?" Most students raise their hands. But then Michael talks about having to work eight hours a day—day in, day out. If you slack off, he says, you get fired. Michael tells his students:

Your job is school. When you take away the free time and the low workload time, what you're left with is about an hour and a half of math and an hour or so of writing. On any given school day, the most you're going to have to work is two and a half hours. If you can't give me the effort for that, how do you expect to get a job for eight hours a day?

That little speech both raises the level of expectations and makes the situation more realistic. And it comes from someone who's "been there."

Empathizing with students serves several purposes: It helps you, the teacher, grasp more accurately the strengths of the student. It helps you appreciate the factors that may be working against those strengths. And it helps the student return the trust, because the student knows that you understand.

In this way, Michael continually focuses on individual students' abilities to make their lives better, building in particular the assets of Personal Power and Positive View of Personal Future. He says that he's turned around a lot of behavior problems by focusing on the positive: pointing out to students their positive attributes and affirming them, encouraging them to find someone on the playground to meet and say something nice to. "I concentrate on being nice to each other and considerate," Michael says, "all the old-school things. . . . In the real world, it's how you treat other people." This emphasis on instilling in his students the ability to take responsibility for their interactions is why Michael says that his students come into the classroom smiling.

In a very real sense, Michael is a natural at this. Pam Christianson, the school family coordinator, says, "It's how he is with kids. It's every day. He's always genuinely concerned, positive with students, staff, and parents. He's a terrific role model. It's contagious. I can't think of a time when he wasn't upbeat and positive." Pam says that because many of Ursa Major's students are in transit as a result of the various assignments of their parents, it's especially critical to engage them quickly. Michael, she says, does that better than anyone.

And for the most part, Michael agrees. "What I do naturally," he says, "is empathize with human beings. I do it really well." And for Michael, that is especially true when it comes to his students. "I'm basically a fifth-grader in a 42-year-old body," says Michael.

Obviously, it takes more than being playful and possessing childlike curiosity to show students understanding, but that's part of it. After all, even Michael will tell you that he doesn't blindly trust that his students will intrinsically want to do well and make the right choices. He has three rules in his classroom:

1. Be respectful, considerate, polite, and a good role model all the time. This will make you proud of yourself and happy.
2. Try to give each task your best effort. Effort is the key to success.
3. Find literature that you love and read as much as you can every day.

To Michael, high expectations are paramount; he's very clear about what he expects from his students. But Michael also lavishes praise on them continually. And he lets them know he's there for them: "I put my arm around them, I give them a good hug, I let them know that I love them."

One student, who comes from a very difficult home life, was reluctant to write a sentence, hardly participated, and frequently ended up in Michael's room as a result of committing some infraction or other. (At Ursa Major, when students misbehave, teachers can send them temporarily to another classroom as sort of a halfway house to the counselor's or principal's office.) One time, Michael approached the student, asked him what was going on, and, after discussing the problem, modeled the behaviors that would help the student, step by step, asking, "What might you do now?" and "Then what would happen?" Within an hour, the student wrote a beautiful paragraph about his situation.

This student still occasionally "shuts down," says Michael, despite all the affirmations about his writing and strategic suggestions for improving it: "Think about if you're going to say a story, and take it sentence by sentence." Just recently, the student had to take a writing assessment, but he didn't get a good night's sleep the night before and couldn't function well enough to write. At the student's request, Michael sent him to the counselor to discuss the situation. The next day, Michael wrote the prompt on the board again, gave the boy a piece of paper, and after an excruciating few moments—"Inside, I had butterflies," says Michael—he started writing.

"It's about figuring out what the kids need, believing that they want to behave and to have structure in their lives," says Michael. "Consistency in any form is a really good thing for them." Michael knows that many of his students' parents come from the military world and as a result sometimes speak *at* them rather than *with* them—conversation often flows one way rather than back and forth, a style unlikely to let anyone feel trusted or motivated. And, in fact, based on students' feedback, as well as his personal experiences, Michael knows that they resent it. It's why he tries to empathize with them and meet them on their own level.

In the end, Michael is successful because he relates with his students and instills trust in them. And he can do that in part because of his own negative school experiences. "I hated school all my life," he says. Now, however, "when I'm here, I'm [at] 150 percent. I love my job. I can't believe how lucky I am."

> > >

trusting teachers give students responsibilities. No one learns responsibility from a book; people learn to be responsible only by being given the opportunity—and choosing to take it. This is the most direct and efficient way that teachers show students they trust them. They say, "Here. I trust you to do this and to do it well." What a great message to give someone! Haven't you yourself felt good when you heard that? Doesn't it motivate you to give a little more of yourself so that you can justify the person's confidence in you?

susie edwards

> GRADE 6

> DE MILLE ELEMENTARY SCHOOL, MIDWAY CITY, CA

"What's it like to be a kid with no mom and no dad, to be staying with someone who doesn't want you?"

That's what Susie Edwards asks herself when she discovers some of the challenges her students face at DeMille Elementary School. A racially mixed community—about a third Asian, a third Latino/Latina, and a third just about everything else—the school of 600 students is just 45 minutes southeast of Los Angeles.

Susie's question is not simply a rhetorical one: One of her students has a parent who is an alcoholic; the other parent is in jail. The student, who lives with his two aunts, doesn't do his homework. When Susie calls him on it, he repeatedly tells her that he has "ADHD" and that he's a "burden" to Susie.

What can a teacher do? One option is to trust that despite his hardships, the boy is capable of succeeding. Susie perceived that the boy was getting negative messages from home. She reached out to him and began to strengthen their relationship—encouraging him to talk, expressing confidence in his abilities, reassuring him that not only did she like him, but she also enjoyed having him around. Now, the boy seeks her out to discuss what's going on in his life—the good, the bad, and the otherwise. And now, Susie has a greater appreciation for him, partly because of what he has to confront every day. As she puts it, "Here I was yelling at him because of his homework," when she had no idea of the larger context of his life. All he wanted, she says, was for "someone to listen to him." As Susie admits, "I'm still learning. There's always something [new] that comes up."

How do you begin to build Developmental Assets with children whose concern for learning is far outweighed by their concern for surviving? How do you learn to understand and trust students whose lives are very different from your own experiences? Susie tries to do what

Michael Walsh does: empathize. Again, it's the first step toward trusting students. "I try to find out where they're coming from," she says. "That's where the relationship begins." But empathizing isn't always easy. That's when Susie employs a second step: giving students responsibilities.

Betty DeWolf, principal of DeMille Elementary, is a big fan of Susie Edwards's teaching methods:

> Students in Susie Edwards's class know what asset building is all about. They can be seen around campus with labels of their individual assets pinned to their shirts—sixth graders proud to share how asset building affects their lives and the choices they make. . . . Susie's at-risk students work together to promote violence prevention by displaying character-development posters and guiding younger students in problem solving through conflict manager activities.

Note: It's Susie's "at-risk" students who are guiding the younger students in problem solving. Susie trusted that these students were capable of teaching others as well as learning themselves, so she gave them responsibilities. They patrol the playground and look for typical problems—students calling each other names or "following" each other. The conflict managers introduce themselves and guide the students through solving their problem: "What did he do that hurt you? How do you think that made the other person feel? What do you think you could do differently? How are we going to prevent this?" Susie says that some of the students are better conflict managers than others, and some of them benefit more than others. Regardless, they all get the message that they're trusted to handle the job.

Susie didn't always have this insight, or the desire to teach, for that matter. Her first career was as a saleswoman in a mom-and-pop clothing store. Gradually, she realized that she "wanted to do something that was important." As with Michael Walsh, school never came easily or naturally to her, so she, too, thought that she might be able to relate to struggling students. She earned her teaching certificate and student-taught at DeMille. She went on to teach fourth grade for four years and then sixth grade.

When she first heard about the Developmental Assets framework, Susie says, "It totally made sense." Since she's very visual, she posted the assets on a bulletin board in her class, and that display has become a centerpiece for student discussions, projects, and other curricular—and extracurricular—activities. Walk into Susie's class, and you might hear her say, "Work with your partners to each identify a personal asset and to choose another asset to develop in yourselves." Once a week, students individually choose assets they want to have or already have, and they write about them. As a St. Patrick's Day assignment that focused on the asset of Interpersonal Competence, students gave each other shamrocks with compliments on them. Susie was so impressed with what her students wrote, she ran to tell the teacher in the classroom next door. For example, one child wrote: "I don't know you very well, but you always have a great smile on your face." "Asset-building moments" such as these reinforce with Susie that her trust in these students' abilities is well deserved.

The issues of trust and responsibility are critical for populations that are traditionally considered "at risk." For example, students from dysfunctional families or communities—with exposure to drug abuse, violence, poverty, and other harmful conditions—don't have much experience with being trusted. (Being neglected is not the same as being trusted.) When students do sense that someone genuinely trusts them, it's liberating, and it dramatically feeds their self-confidence. It's often more of a leap for teachers to bestow that trust by giving the students responsibilities. After all, some may say, "What have students done to earn it?"

This latter question bears some thought, and it spawns other questions. Do students, in fact, have to earn your trust? If they must, how can they earn it? If they've never been given responsibilities, how can they be expected to show that they're responsible? If your students were to begin a relationship with someone, what would you advise them about trusting the other person?

There are no simple answers. But asking the questions may guide you to a policy that's appropriate for each student. Susie typically makes the first move with a student because she thinks it will help her understand that student. She'd probably say that all young people deserve your trust until they do something that negates it. It's like being innocent until proven guilty. And if they do betray her trust, Susie believes in giving her students a second—and a third, and a fourth—chance. Students showing that they care—about her, about school, about the process—regain her trust quickly.

Besides, Susie will also tell you that the positiveness of an asset-building approach has made at least as much of a difference with her as with her students. If she's having a problem with a student, she'll try to turn it around and focus on that student's strengths. And whenever students are referred to the principal for behavior problems, those students bring along a list of their strengths, so the principal can point out "the good stuff" as well as the "bad." "I want a positive atmosphere," she says. "You end up on a nice note when you walk away from them." Think about how important that is, especially to "at-risk" students: They have a conflict with someone and still walk away feeling good about themselves and about the other person.

Principal DeWolf tells the story about one of Susie's students who was being harassed. The only reason Susie found out about it—the bully was careful not to do anything around teachers or large groups—was that some of the victim's classmates let her know. Susie took several tacks: She discussed the general issue of bullying during the class "Community Circle" time; she addressed bullying through videos, skill building, journal writing, and other activities; and she met privately with the two boys involved. The most difficult part, says DeWolf, was getting the victim to admit being a victim. At one point, the boy began acting like a bully himself.

By the end of the year, however, with Susie continually working with him to build his assets, the boy owned up to being both a victim and a bully and began finding a more comfortable place within the school community. All through the process, Susie emphasized the boy's strengths, gave him the responsibility to reach his own insights, and trusted that he would indeed accomplish that.

If Susie's relationships with her students begin with knowledge, then they're sustained by her trusting them in the classroom. She starts off with a clean slate for all her students, regardless of their history with other teachers: "I don't look at the past. I don't want to hear any stories." The first week of school sets the tone for the entire year. "It's kind of a cliché," she says, "but at the beginning of the school year, we start off making rules together. The first week of school is so important. . . . When [the students] feel as if they own something—it's *our* classroom, not my classroom."

During that crucial first week, all her students get to know each other, set boundaries, and write their communal goals on a poster. What do they want their classroom to be like? (Last year, they wanted a place to feel comfortable and to make friends.) At the end of the year, they check the poster to see the extent to which they met their goals and expectations. All during the year, Susie gives them responsibilities— from the mundane (they use hand signals to leave the room for bathroom breaks and are acknowledged with nothing more than a nod) to the more notable (the conflict managers).

For the most part, her students thrive, though Susie has had her share of what she calls *failures*. One student got suspended twice and finally expelled for rudeness and other behavior problems. She'd had numerous talks with him, telling him that he was ultimately responsible for getting himself in trouble. He kept promising to change, but he didn't follow through. "I couldn't believe anything he said," says Susie. The boy had a rough family life as well as a learning disability, and she couldn't get him to join the community in the classroom. It was a tough situation, says Susie. Still, the successes are plentiful—students who respond to her when they had difficulty responding in previous years, students who have "found themselves" after having been given responsibilities, students who end up contributing to the classroom more than they ever thought they would.

Debra Hill thinks she knows why. Debra is the prevention and child welfare and attendance coordinator, as well as the asset trainer, for the school district. She's had a lot of experience with Susie in prevention meetings, asset trainings, and other activities. Debra marvels at Susie's infectiously upbeat philosophy:

> *Susie is always so surprised to hear about anything negative relating to her students. She always reframes it: "You know, in the classroom he's always very helpful and responsive. He's really a leader." She brings the child out in light of his strengths. You can tell there's a connection with the students. The students feel cared for.*

Debra remembers Susie trying "20 ways" to get a student to go to an overnight science camp. She kept telling him, "I don't want you to miss out on this." It turned out that he was afraid to spend the night away from his parents. Susie worked with his family to encourage him to take the risk.

It's all very basic to Susie: "If the kids are happy, the better behaved they will be, and learning becomes easier." Susie considers herself a "dreamer." She wants, she says, a "Magic School Bus kind of classroom, where students are having fun and learning, too"—the classroom that as a child, she would have wanted herself.

> > >

trusting teachers challenge students. Challenging students isn't the same as daring students, and it's more than giving them responsibilities. Challenging students is pushing them just a little past what they think they can do; it's helping them close the gap to their potential. This part can be tricky; you don't want to frustrate students, but you also don't want to let them coast. It's one of the jobs of a teacher to challenge students and to trust that they can do better than they already have.

kathi swanson

> GRADE 6
> LOWER MACUNGIE MIDDLE SCHOOL, MACUNGIE, PA

Is trust instinctive, or do you have to work at it? Do you trust on the basis of your feelings or your rational thoughts?

Many teachers would like to be spontaneously trusting, they'd like to give students more responsibility, but they're afraid; what if their students don't measure up? With the teachers in this book, however, the consensus is clear: the upside of trusting more than compensates for the downside of "failing." Sometimes, you just have to take the plunge.

Kathi Swanson took the plunge. Her students say it best:

I was in her class last year. Mrs. Swanson really takes her time explaining things, but doesn't talk down to you. She speaks to you as if you were an adult. I really like the way she was able to get me interested about whatever subject she was teaching by giving a lot of examples. Mrs. Swanson introduced me to a book series that I can't stop reading. Her high expectations and enthusiasm motivated me to give 110 percent. Mrs. Swanson is my favorite teacher ever.

MAX, FORMER STUDENT

Most teachers get annoyed at me because I ask a lot of questions. Mrs. Swanson doesn't care. She always answers all my questions and never limits me to what I can and can't ask. Mrs. Swanson never looks down on our class. She always treats us how we would like to be treated, not like a kindergartner. I think that Mrs. Swanson is a very awesome teacher.

CAROLYN, CURRENT STUDENT

When you talk to people about Kathi Swanson, one theme emerges more than any other: how Kathi trusts students to excel. In order for her to do that, she has to know her students' capabilities. And the primary reason Kathi knows her students' capabilities? "I just think she really listens to the kids," says Karen Shade, secretary at Lower Macungie Middle. Karen has seen that firsthand. One afternoon, after 4 P.M., a girl was sitting in the office with a problem. Kathi came into the office, sat down beside the girl—not one of "her" students, mind you—and listened to her until her mother came for her.

But it's not only listening: It's challenging students to do more than they think they can do, and maybe even more than *you* think they can do. Several years ago, Kathi's fifth-grade students wanted to start their own school-supplies store, and Kathi helped it happen. First, of course, she and the students had to ask the principal for permission to run the store. Kathi had thought that the principal would deny the request. When he told her and her students, "This is a great idea," her mouth dropped, she says.

Kathi went to work with her students—poring through catalogs, raising money by going to the parent-teacher organization and getting a $250 loan to be repaid in six months, calculating inventories, facilitating scheduling, pricing and testing products, writing résumés, and assigning jobs in the store. For two months, she guided her students in all phases of the store, including surveying other students about what they might purchase, developing a list of materials, and making graphs about projected sales. Students even developed a code of ethics. ("You shouldn't eat while you're working.") The store was a rousing success, and the students repaid the loan in three months. The trust paid off. The assigning of responsibilities paid off. The support and encouragement paid off.

Imagine all the things that might go wrong in a project like this! It might bog down and disrupt the rest of the curriculum. Students might get bored. You might have to spend endless hours correcting their mistakes. You might even lose money! But with careful tutorship, continual monitoring, and appropriately apportioned praise, projects like these succeed because of—not despite—students' assumption of a good deal of the responsibility.

What does it take for a teacher to trust that students can achieve in this way? What does it take for students to believe that their teacher trusts them? "She's very honest, very down-to-earth, very approachable, and her students feel those things," says Alison Saeger Panik, a former colleague. "She doesn't have a wall between her and kids."

Kathi says that she deliberately challenges her students. When she knows that she's going to be gone for a day or so—for example, to present at a conference—she asks for students to take on jobs that she knows are "big deals" to them: taking attendance, answering the phone, making sure that the television is on for announcements, distributing hall passes, keeping records. She helps them brainstorm other tasks that need to be done while she's away. She'll even rehearse with some of them so that they're prepared to do their jobs. On one occasion, she even developed an application form, and students wrote in their names, date, the types of jobs they were interested in, and the reasons they thought Kathi should "hire" them.

Trusting students to assume responsibility pervades Kathi's classes. During one class, Kathi let students hold their own discussion of slavery. At the beginning, Kathi participated, but eventually, she just stepped back and let her students take over. This could happen only if you challenged your students to handle the extra responsibility and learn more from you and each other than from you alone. Concurrently, this could happen only if you challenged yourself to stay back and observe.

Kathi knew from the time she was in second grade that she was up for the challenge of being a teacher. Even then, she thought, "I could do this better," or "They missed something," or "They could have done it this way." But she was disappointed after she got her first job teaching sixth grade in Elgin, Illinois, a suburb of Chicago. "It was really hard," she says. She was only 21; she'd led a middle-class life, and many of her students hadn't. She became frustrated because she neither understood them nor was able to reach them.

Eventually, she moved to New Jersey and taught kindergarten for a year and a half. There, with six-year-old learning curves being steep and dramatic, she could watch her students learn something every day: "It was visible," she says. Kathi soon felt compelled to return home to Pennsylvania, where she's been teaching ever since—first, elementary school, and for the last three years, middle school, where she has become a popular role model and students seek her out.

What's made the difference? When Kathi began teaching middle school, she chose to make connections with students who were having trouble with transitions—so she and they could transition together. Middle school needs are different, says Kathi. Students are almost but not quite adult, so she has to allow herself, as she puts it, "to believe in what they're doing and let them know that."

That strategy is evidently working: Children gravitate toward Kathi. "One year," she says, "the kids who were always in trouble seemed to find me." One troubled boy whom no one else wanted in class would skip lunch to have math class with her—a class that was two grades lower than his—and ask her if there was any way he could help her. The boy loved art, so Kathi entrusted him to design a sign for her door. She took the risk to purposely connect with someone who desperately needed to be recognized for the things he did well.

Connections are important to Kathi—not only connections between students and her but also between students and other adults. A few of Kathi's students wondered why parents who didn't care about their schoolwork still had to sign their papers. Kathi and her co-teacher devised an asset-rich alternative: They told the students that, as a substitute for their parents, they could get at least three adults at school to sign their work—and they would receive bonus points for securing the signatures. Kathi selected and alerted the adults, and the students went about establishing connections.

The secretary, Karen, was one of those adults; she got to know plenty of students she wouldn't have otherwise met. This year, those students are in the seventh grade; she says hi to them in the hallway, and they say hi to her. The little things make a difference—to both student and adult.

When Carolyn (one of the students who was quoted earlier) transferred into the district at the beginning of the year, she didn't know anyone in her class. "But after the first day of school, she never looked back or regretted the move," says her mother, Mary, who goes into the classroom once a week to help with paperwork so Kathi can focus on teaching. Why? Because, explains Mary, "Kathi somehow seems to find a way to talk to the kids that simultaneously rewards them for their achievements and yet encourages them to strive for more."

Max, the student who said that Kathi introduced him to a book series that he couldn't stop reading, had a similar experience. Until Kathi introduced him to Lemony Snicket's A Series of Unfortunate Events books, he'd always believed that he was a poor student and that he couldn't read. Max, who has Tourette's syndrome, read all of them. Then Kathi introduced him to J. K. Rowling's Harry Potter books. Max read all of them. Kathi was the first person Max excitedly ran to after he "graduated" out of the Instructional Support Group into which he'd been placed. Max is now in the eighth grade and a member of the National Junior Honor Society; he drops by Kathi's classroom to tell her about new books coming out. For her part, Kathi is now the building's literacy reading coach. She assures students who don't like to read that they just haven't found the right book yet.

It's these connections —borne of Kathi's laying down challenges and students accepting them—that bring students back to Kathi again and again. They e-mail her. They call her up. They go to the movies with her. And she encourages them all—current and former students.

Another parent, Ron, sings the praises of Kathi on behalf of his daughter, Alyssa. He recalls the time that Alyssa and her best friend, Julie, had a falling out. Kathi recognized that the girls weren't behaving as usual, he explains, and brought them together for a talk, challenging them to solve their own conflict and spurring them to come up with solutions: "What do you think is going on? What do you think you should do?" The girls were able to resolve their issues, says Ron, thanks to Kathi, who "stepped out of the norm to assist."

That seems to *be* the norm with Kathi. Ron himself witnessed "Story Time," a day in the early winter when students were asked to come to school in pajamas or other comfortable sleepwear. When he arrived at Kathi's classroom, he says,

I was quite surprised to see the room had been transformed into a warm, comfortable living room—the students dressed in their comfort wear, their sleeping bags or blankets laid in organized groups on the floor, and a whole host of reading material scattered throughout. Mrs. Swanson started the festivities by reading a memorable story from her past. The story lasted about 15 minutes, and I watched as the students offered no distraction and were mesmerized by her every word. . . . It's not often that you get to hear your teacher in a warm, long, plaid bathrobe, sitting in a rocking chair with a reading light hovering over her shoulder. That's the stuff memories are made of—lasting impressions.

There are burdens, of course. "If there's somebody I'm not getting through to," Kathi says, it wears on her. If she's working with colleagues "who don't love the job the same way I do," it wears on her. Teaching is not for everyone, says Kathi; "it has to be in their gut." Kathi has concluded that it's the people who want to connect with students who make the best teachers.

"Students need to feel that adults in school want them there," adds Kathi. And she knows, now more than ever, how critical her role is in instilling that feeling. Just recently, a former student dropped in to visit her. Now a junior, the girl was Kathi's student six years ago. After they had talked for a while, the student showed Kathi that she had kept every single memo, note, and bit of feedback that Kathi had written to her; it had all given her the confidence she needed in ensuing years.

It floored Kathi to realize what an impact she'd made—and how her influence could have made a difference in either direction. "What if I had written something negative?" she asked. "How scary is that?"

> > >

trusting teachers give up control. Empathizing with students is one thing, but giving them responsibilities, challenging them to do more—that requires you to step back a little. Just as your students can gain more confidence by assuming more control, you can gain more trust in them by relinquishing some of your control. Regardless of the age of the students, there's a significant difference between helping them do something and letting them do it. When students are given the freedom to succeed or fail, it's like giving them the feeling of riding a bicycle for the first time without their parent's hand on their shoulder. And isn't this what you strive for as a teacher, to give your students the information and skills so that they can make good decisions on their own? When you give up control, you're trusting that what you've done for your students has taken hold.

susan cressey

> GRADE 9
> KENNEBUNK HIGH SCHOOL, KENNEBUNK, ME

By her own admission, the biggest compliment Susan Cressey ever received was when someone told her that she behaved the same with students in the classroom as she did with adults outside the classroom. It's important to Susan to be who she is wherever she is, and it doesn't seem as if she's had much difficulty accomplishing that.

For Susan in the classroom, it's not a matter of who has control; it's a matter of students and teacher working together to achieve goals. She believes that goals can be achieved together. She doesn't have to put on her "authoritarian" or "disciplinarian" hat to wrest control from students. It's the confidence she has in herself that allows her to cede control when it's appropriate.

On the face of it, Sue simply teaches ninth-grade English and also takes on some administrative duties at Kennebunk High School, a small, 900-student school in rural Maine. But she does so much more than that. In fact, when she was selected to be principal of the school three years ago, she turned down the offer because she wanted to teach. As the current principal, Nelson Beaudoin, says of her, "Her room becomes a hangout for students before and after school, both as a place where learning expectations are met and friendships and bonding occur. She works with each student to connect them to what they need. . . . She takes the success of each student personally."

And she trusts that they will succeed. The students she has taught can attest to that firsthand:

> *During my sophomore year of high school, I still had not experienced any sort of involvement with extracurricular activities. I was surprised when Mrs. Cressey approached me at this time to fill a leadership position in a new program at Kennebunk High School called KHS Connections. She and a junior student had designed this program to ease the freshmen transition into high school, and they asked me to come on board. I had experienced leadership opportunities before, but never within the school, so this was my first taste of power, and indeed, I did feel like I had power. Instead of ruling over everything, I learned quickly how fair Mrs. Cressey is, and how she really lets students take responsibility. She made me feel like I had a place within the school, by letting me share opinions about the program and take actions for change. Once she allowed me to realize that I could instigate change within my own school, I quickly started to pick up other activities because I wasn't shy anymore. Mrs. Cressey really helped me to open up and find my place by offering me one opportunity in the high school.*
>
> **SARAH, FORMER STUDENT**

Susan herself says that giving up control was difficult at first, but as she got more confident, she realized that the most rewarding way to teach was when, for example, students worked on a project and she didn't have to worry as much about the management. "It takes a lot of planning," she says, "but when you're able to stand in the back of the room and students are excited—to me, that's success." So now there are advisory groups and student forums. Students make decisions on their own, sometimes inviting administrators to talk to them.

Some teachers find the idea of giving up control to students difficult. Why is that? What negative things might happen if you gave students control?

> The students could fail and then lose the incentive to take control in the future.
> You could view the students' failure as your failure and then lose the incentive to give them control in the future.
> The whole process of letting go may make you more than a little uneasy.

If you're uneasy about the process of letting go—*that* you may have to work on. When giving up control reaps dividends, you'll be rewarded. Understand that Susan has been teaching for 31 years, and you might be surprised that she was open to such change. But the Developmental Assets framework helped, as it resonated immediately with Susan when she first heard of it only a few years ago. "I thought, 'Yes, this is what I do; this is what works with kids.'" Since then, she has strived to make the building of assets as *intentional* as possible.

For example, Susan joined a DART (Developing Assets and Relationships Together) group and, according to her former student Sarah,

takes the assets that our team is based on very seriously. . . . She allows students to find their voice and responsibility both inside and out of DART. At our DART meetings, she is always curious to learn what students think and is always ready to volunteer new ideas about how we can improve certain aspects of our school-community relationship.

At one of DART's monthly discussions this year, students talked about the kinds of decisions they had to make in their daily lives and encouraged adults to incorporate the topic of decision making into their advisory program for sophomores. Susan was impressed with these decisions. Even considering, she says, that the students are sensible and

Kennebunk seems safe, they still have to decide about sex, drug use, peer pressure, college, and a whole host of other issues.

DART has also conducted a survey about the relationships between local police and teenagers. As a result of the survey, the police department realized that it could best achieve good relationships with teenagers by actually discussing issues with them in a nonthreatening environment; the upshot is that now a representative from the police department attends DART meetings. More and more students are becoming involved with DART, and more and more students are saying that they like school. The goal of all these activities, of course, is for the students to make a positive difference in their school, to leave it a better place than when they came.

Kennebunk High School guidance counselor Dick Farnsworth mentions something else that's often critical in the development of a teenager: recognition. Susan, he points out, "showcases" students by having them share their interests and achievements with staff. To an adult, that may seem like nothing more than people giving a show-and-tell about things they like, but to a teenager, it's official recognition and validation that what they're interested in and what they've accomplished has value. As Dick says, "It's so refreshing to see these particular students having an opportunity to really shine and to be superstars for a day!"

Asset building doesn't happen by just making students feel good, however, says Susan. "In the classroom, for example, the curriculum needs to be rigorous and praise needs to be authentic. Hard work that is well done builds confidence."

Much of what Susan does depends on her ability to place trust in her students. Even though Susan admits that giving up some control has been difficult, she still does it because she recognizes that both she and her students benefit from it.

Teachers giving up control is not a common occurrence. That's why many people find it astonishing when it's revealed, for example, that "students managed this entire project by themselves" or that "she drew up her own contract and assessed her progress each week" or that "he rallied his classmates to support the petition with a fund-raising effort." People marvel when youth do something that adults find routine.

We see many more examples of the *lack* of trust: Students may have opinions, but they're only advisory. Students may participate in projects, but they have to defer to the adult manager. Part of this has to do with adults genuinely not wanting students to fail. But a lot of it has to do with adults' meager experience in giving students responsibility—to succeed or to fail.

Whether you're an adult or a young person, you need trust in order to build Developmental Assets. Assets aren't something teachers can just pour into students' ears; students have to *do* something, they have to be involved. As Susan says, "A good teacher internalizes the assets and does them naturally. If your focus is doing what's best for kids, you're always looking for ways to get them involved. You walk the talk."

Susan's general strategy for "walking her talk" and involving students is very basic, and it's one you'll hear repeated throughout this book: She gets to know them. She finds out what they're interested in, whether through them or their families. She tries to make connections between their interests and her curriculum. She gives students two or three choices to make, then slowly increases their responsibilities— to choosing topics for an opinion paper or books to read for reports. "High school's a time when they need to practice making decisions," says Susan. Gradually, she creates the climate she's aiming for: working together.

Getting students to embrace that goal is not always so easy. One year Susan taught a class of mostly freshmen boys, including some special-needs students; they didn't like reading, writing, or school in general. They also couldn't sit still. No matter what Susan tried, it seemed as if the boys fed off each other's energy to resist her attempts to teach them. Susan concluded that modeling from higher-achieving students might be in order. As a result, next year the school won't track students academically; instead, it will provide heterogeneous classes so that under-achieving students can get support from their classmates. That way, the entire class really will be working together—to learn.

The successes more than compensate for the struggles. Recently, Susan set up her class as if it were a science fair: Students chose topics they were interested in and reported on them. One boy with a history of troubles and poor academic performance was at school by 7 in the morning to set up his display on mountain biking, a sport that he loves. He turned in the written component of his assignment, and he made eye contact when he was presenting his report. He received praise from both his peers and adults.

Three ingredients contributed to this boy's success: his delight in being able to talk about something he was already involved in; Susan's trust that he could succeed; and her willingness to let him control his report. "Every student has something they do well," says Susan. "It's a matter of letting them know you believe in them."

One of Susan's students who definitely got that message is Eileen. When Eileen graduated, among other things, Susan had arranged for her to tutor two freshman boys—Tom and Steve—and believes that as a result, she inspired Eileen to consider teaching as a career. Eileen wrote Susan the following note:

> *Mrs. Cressey,*
>
> *At my sister's graduation from Harvard, the president of the school gave a very compelling speech. His overall theme was to provide equal-opportunity higher education. He felt that too often kids get overlooked in public schools and are not being encouraged to challenge themselves and succeed.*
>
> *"The battles of America's future are won and lost in today's public schools."*
>
> *As I sat and listened to his speech, I couldn't help but think of you. You are on the front line of such battles every day. I have witnessed you impacting and changing lives as well as been the receiver of your kindness and constant support. I never felt that I would miss KHS or even be missed, but after this year and after meeting Tom and Steve, I know that I did not waste a minute of*

*high school and even had the honor of leaving a tiny bit of me
behind.*

*Thank you for letting me have the chance to fight next to you
in your daily battles. You truly make a difference.*

Love,

Eileen

I will miss you so much.

Not all your students will grow up to be teachers. But no matter
what students do in the future, one thing they will have to learn is
to take control and accept responsibility. And if you attempt to teach
them that, then you'll have succeeded as well.

Prepare them to accept responsibility. Express your trust in them.
Give them the tools they need to succeed—and the opportunity to
use those tools themselves. Have them set their goals high enough to
be meaningful yet realistic enough to be achievable. Be ready to help.
And in the end, praise them for their efforts and for whatever they did
achieve. Help them not to label their effort a failure; help them take
away from the experience more knowledge and more skills, so that they
exceed their achievement the next time.

Susan Cressey does all of these things. And for her students, that
makes all the difference.

engaging
teachers

> By allowing the students to come in my room to listen to music
> and interact during lunch recess, I was able to experience
> something more awesome than ever before. I sat back and
> watched students with a large variety of interests
> and abilities come together on equal ground.

MINDY ELLERBEE

engaging teachers make learning fun in different and interesting ways. Mindy Ellerbee has her students analyze fictional characters in terms of assets. Beth Grove turns her classroom into a Chinese tableau to show parents what her students know about Chinese history. Tom Kidd facilitates student discussions on topics that relate to family and friends. And during a unit on the Vietnam War, Andrea Godfrey Brown takes her students to a cemetery.

The teachers in this section make students want to come to school. They establish connections between themselves and their students and between their students and their coursework. Teachers who engage students instill *in them the priceless gift of the desire to learn. How fundamental, how critical that is! When young people are amused, intrigued, stimulated, or challenged by what they're learning, they want to learn more; that desire to learn then transfers to other subjects. The young person becomes a true student.*

While engaging teachers easily build the asset of School Engagement, they also help build others as well: High Expectations, Creative Activities, Achievement Motivation, Reading for Pleasure, Sense of Purpose, and even Service to Others. Besides benefiting from the cumulative effect of building assets, the students of these teachers know that learning isn't just memorization, knowledge isn't just facts, and topics aren't just assignments. They know that they can enjoy learning and that they can often use what they learn.

As in the previous section, here's a challenge: Read about the ways these teachers engage their students, and then think about the ways you engage your *students. What can you do to make their learning more meaningful, more relevant, more enjoyable?*

> > >

ngaging teachers make the curriculum interesting. You can probably remember sitting glassy-eyed in one classroom or another,
benumbed by the incessant droning of your teacher, vaguely cognizant
of a deluge of facts that you could surely memorize—if only you cared
enough to do it. Classrooms don't have to be like that. Engaging teachers use a variety of strategies to draw their students into the lessons.
Some of these strategies involve technology, such as video and DVD
players, computers, and interactive whiteboards. But other strategies
involve using imagination. When you have the ability to transmit information in a way that's provocative, relevant, and entertaining, you are
an engaging teacher.

mindy ellerbee

> GRADE 5
> WILLIAMS ELEMENTARY SCHOOL, GEORGETOWN, TX

Mindy Ellerbee's sisters and older brother are all educators. When she
saw her brother not only making learning fun for his high school biology
students but also having a great rapport with them, she thought, "I can
do that."

Inspired, Mindy earned her degree and began teaching almost
immediately, at age 22. A year later, however, she started to feel that
she didn't have enough patience for the job, so she left education and
became a flight attendant. On these flights, she slowly discovered she'd
been questioning children about why they weren't in school. Four years
after leaving the classroom, Mindy returned to a career in education,
teaching in an after-school program and mentoring younger children
at Benold Middle School in Georgetown, Texas.

Shortly after the violence at Columbine High School, Mindy attended
a Search Institute conference in Colorado and heard students express
how important it is to know that adults care about them. While at the
conference, says Mindy, she called her mother, somewhat emotionally,

to thank her "for setting boundaries and expectations and for always being accessible" to her. Her own parents were always there for her, she says, always encouraged her to achieve whatever she thought she could achieve, and never judged her.

That was six years ago. Mindy realized at that moment that she needed to be an asset builder for children, just as her parents were asset builders for her. "I had no idea I was so blessed," she says now.

After returning from that fateful conference in Colorado, Mindy educated herself on the Developmental Assets and then started communicating them to her students. Once she did that, she naturally started to hear the assets in stories. Her students read novels and examined the characters' relationships with their parents and other adults. For example, in *Summer of the Monkeys*, written by Wilson Rawls, the 14-year-old protagonist doesn't have confidence in himself; he depends on his grandfather for support. He's selfish, but as he develops, he recognizes his parents' influence on him. Mindy's students identify with the novel's characters and write about them, comparing themselves with the characters. "All strong characters have assets," says Mindy. And whenever she reads aloud, she asks, "What assets does this character have?" She operates on the theory that if students recognize the assets as good things in others, they'll try to build those assets in themselves.

This works especially well with external assets, such as Family Support. After discussing the stories, students write a letter to an adult who has been supportive of them—a parent, a relative, a neighbor, a teacher. They talk about the responsibilities of being a supporter, and the discussion segues into how they can support others.

Mindy teaches fifth-grade language arts (as well as social studies, life skills, and homeroom) at Williams Elementary School, also in Georgetown. Language arts is the focus of the class, but Developmental Assets are pervasive, too. When Mindy incorporates assets into her teaching, she accomplishes several things:

> She transcends the specific reading matter so that students can transfer what they've learned to other reading matter.

> She relates the academic content to students' lives so that students can apply what they've learned to situations outside the classroom.
> She engages students so that they're motivated to participate in the current lesson as well as in future lessons.
> She builds specific assets.
> She learns more about her students so that she can build better relationships with each of them.

If you believe that it's a lot of work to integrate Developmental Assets into your curriculum, think about what Mindy does. Think about how much easier it is to teach when you know that your students are interested in learning. Think about how much easier it is to manage your classroom when you know that your students get along with one another and have consistent goals.

Mindy also uses other creative strategies—such as music—to build assets as well as to teach students about the assets. Some of the songs she plays for students as a springboard to discussions of assets are "Still on Your Side" (BBMak), "What If" (Creed), "Livin' on a Prayer" (Bon Jovi), "The Dance" (Garth Brooks), "I'll Be" (Reba McEntire), "Survivor" (Destiny's Child), "Peace Train" (Cat Stevens), and "It's My Life" (Crush).

For example, the opening lyrics from "Still on Your Side" talk about a friend's caring and support.

As students listen to the song, they write phrases that stick out for them; Mindy does the same on the board. Following that, Mindy facilitates a discussion about the theme of the song so that students can more fully understand the lyrics. Then she plays the song again, and this time students relate the song to themselves. They imagine singing it to someone or someone singing it to them. The activity alternates between the asset-based ideas of support and empowerment.

Discussing music and identifying with fictional characters allows students to draw parallels to their own lives. These types of lessons make a significant impression, because the Developmental Assets have a multiplier effect: If learning about something resonates with young people, then they'll pass it on. And learning about assets definitely resonates with young people, as you can tell from listening to some of Mindy's students:

> *I think it is very important to be an asset builder because if kids like us didn't talk or just say hi to someone that doesn't or does have many friends, then that person will have an empty place in his or her heart because parents can't be the only asset builder in one's life. The kids have to have friends to feel like they're wanted. By doing that it will make that kid feel so good and warm inside and you will feel good about yourself for doing that, because you've touched somebody where no one else has.*

> > >

> *Some of my friends are saying that I've changed . . . and I say, "A good change or a bad change?" They always say a good change. I say, "How?" They say I didn't talk very much and now I can't stop.*

> > >

> *I know you shouldn't have to be told to stick up for someone; you should just do it anyway, because I hear people being put down every day. Like during seventh period, I heard someone get put down, but not to their face. The person said it to me and I said, "You shouldn't say that." And the kid just walked on. And now I know he is not a really good friend. I know because people make fun of my birthmark a lot.*

> > >

> *It is important to receive the assets because I think it makes a part of who you are and how you act. If I didn't have the assets, I would probably be rude, mean, and go saying whatever I wanted to whoever I wanted. But with the assets, it kinda teaches you how to act, respect people, and how to react to certain things or problems. . . . It gives you the chance to teach someone something right. Also, if you do teach them, you might change how they treat people.*

What you can tell from these quotations is that students *learned* the topic; they *applied* the topic to their lives; and they *enjoyed* doing it. That's the essence of engagement.

Mindy's principal, Cheryl Lang, says that Mindy models and teaches the 40 Developmental Assets daily in and out of the classroom:

> *She provides support for her students through the positive, caring relationship that she creates with all students. She especially reaches out to students who may not have home support systems or other external assets available to them.*

Colleague Terri Boccella also highlights Mindy's building of assets:

> *Mindy is such a natural at instantly establishing relationships with her students at the beginning of a new school year. This is the basis for her success as a teacher as well as [an] asset builder. She is known by all to be a nurturing, supportive, and empowering teacher. . . . She has high expectations of mutual respect with the students. They know that she values them, and they in turn show her respect and work hard for her.*

Mindy makes a safe, comfortable classroom environment a priority, since feelings of anxiety can be a barrier to engagement. If her students have a question, she explains, "no matter how ridiculous it may sound to someone else, it's okay. You can't get engagement unless the students know they'll be respected—by their teachers and their peers." Some students have a fear of reading aloud, so in order to get them to focus, she shares a story about herself when *she* was young. She, too, had panicked about reading aloud. Mindy's goal is for all her students to be involved in what everyone is reading; if they feel uneasy reading that particular day, then they can do it the next time. She makes her classroom safe and comfortable so that students enjoy the work.

To make this happen, Mindy displays a sign of the Developmental Assets in her classroom and makes sure that students understand the four categories of the external assets in particular (Support, Empowerment, Boundaries and Expectations, and Constructive Use of Time). She wants students to see that they can be asset builders. "Just because they're 11 years old doesn't mean that they can't model good listening, support someone, et cetera," says Mindy. The students respond; they learn about the assets and then begin to build them for and with others. Sometimes students from previous years come back to her classroom and talk about students who "lack assets."

In *Building Assets Together* (1997, Search Institute), Jolene Roehlke-partain presents an activity called "Golden Nuggets" as a way to introduce the asset category of Empowerment. Mindy adapts the activity to also build the assets of Caring School Climate, Bonding to School, and Interpersonal Competence.

Each student is given a rock. The rocks are of various sizes; some are old, others dirty, still others shiny. In teams of four, students get opportunities to share which rock they would "listen to" the most and then order them in terms of value.

As a team, students choose the most valuable rock to share with the class. Some students say that the smallest rock is the most valuable because it's a child, and it should be listened to so its feelings won't be hurt. Some students say that a rock with many sides will be able to see all sides of a problem. Some students say that round rocks let things roll off them and won't stay angry if you take your anger out on them. Some students say that larger, older rocks have more knowledge. Some students choose the prettier rocks because of the way they look.

The students are then told that there is gold inside the rocks and are given a chance to change the order of the rocks, if they wish. Most of the teams move the largest rocks up to the most valuable position.

Mindy closes the lesson by saying that all the rocks have the same amount of gold in them, because the gold is at the heart of the rock, and we don't know the rocks' true value until we take the time to talk and find out. She asks students to say hello to other students they don't know. Mindy says that the behavior tends to spread throughout the school, until by the end of the day, everyone is smiling and saying hello in the hall, in the cafeteria, and in classrooms.

The focus on Developmental Assets has made a change in Mindy as well as in her students. In the past, she was very strict, giving misbehaving students a scornful glance that she says she inherited from her mother. "Students would stop whatever they were doing," she says, without pride. One quiet, intelligent boy called her "Medusa," saying that whenever she gives them that look, "We freeze in our spot." "Medusa" became Mindy's not-very-welcome nickname.

But as she became more familiar with the assets, Mindy realized how important it is to be approachable. She accordingly changed her style. Now, in fact, she says that "my greatest fault" is getting too personally involved; she's working on learning how to say no and setting her own boundaries. People open up to her, yet at times she feels that she has to draw lines and may say, "I'm sorry this has happened to you, but would it be okay for me to refer you to the counselor?"

Mindy learned this the hard way. When she was first starting to build Developmental Assets in middle school, some of the students formed a small, informal group in which they'd join Mindy for lunch, music, and talk. Mindy provided such a warm, friendly environment that the group grew and grew until it became the size of a small class. "I loved it," says Mindy. Popular students, unpopular students—the entire gamut would come in and talk with each other. They all felt protected; they all felt supported, explains Mindy. But, she adds, other teachers became concerned and said students were coming into their classrooms feeling distracted by the discussions. The administrators at the time didn't back her and Mindy ended the group.

Mindy realizes now that she should have first involved the other teachers in some way. Now she shares everything with her fellow teachers—to the extent that by the end of this year, all the fifth graders in Williams Elementary will be versed in the asset framework. Her principal supports her, her colleagues support her, and Mindy knows that what she's doing is accepted.

Still, as any teacher reading this book will know, it can be tough. "The most frustration a teacher will experience," says Mindy, "is that they will not see immediate results." Just this year, three of her students were "incredible discipline problems," and she persisted in trying to build their assets. One boy moved away, the second hasn't changed significantly, and the third blossomed. "You just hope that something you did was in some small way responsible for their success," Mindy says. "You can't give up."

Here's the real payoff: A former student whom Mindy taught in fifth grade became her high school's valedictorian. On the occasion, the girl wrote Mindy a note, saying, "I'm going to be an educator because of you." Mindy has a photo of that student and her graduation announcement framed on her wall. If for any reason she finds herself getting on edge, focusing on the negative instead of the positive, or turning back into Medusa, she has that reminder about what can happen when she builds assets for and with her students. And that makes it all worthwhile.

> > >

engaging teachers relate the curriculum to students. How can you relate a standard curriculum to each of your students? It can be done. It has been done. Sometimes, it takes knowing your students well enough that you can adapt activities to each of their interests. But more often, it's a matter of making the activities more open-ended, so that students contribute whatever's the most relevant, the most personal. You give them the tools and they paint the picture. Engaging teachers allow students to own the curriculum and to take its lessons outside the classroom.

beth grove

> GRADE 6
> O'NEILL ELEMENTARY SCHOOL, MISSION VIEJO, CA

Meeting established learning standards is important for any great teacher, but that's not all of what great teaching is for Beth Grove. As she puts it, "I'm [even] more worried about what kinds of human beings [my students] are when they walk outside the classroom. . . . I'm constantly trying to adjust to make [content] more meaningful to them, make them want to be here." So how does she make the curriculum interesting to students? She relates it directly to them.

In a unit about oral histories, for example, students ask adults— family members, neighbors—to tell them stories that they can then relate to the class. They also get family recipes, learn interviewing skills, and make a collage. Then they bring the person to school and tell their favorite part about interviewing them. It's a great idea: It involves students' families in their learning. It increases the likelihood that students will learn the unit. It focuses many of the older people in the community on what many of the younger people in the community are learning. The lesson is: Projects that extend beyond the classroom into students' lives will more likely engage them in learning.

For Beth, helping to engage students by also helping to build assets doesn't take any more time. She puts it well: "If you give more, you get more back." Her aspiration? To be the same kind of teacher that she wants her children to have, and using the Developmental Assets is a great way to accomplish that.

But all students don't learn the same way; in that respect, Beth believes that her greatest challenge in achieving her goal is providing individualized instruction—recognizing students' various learning styles and modifying her own teaching to accommodate them. From the very beginning of the year, Beth tries to figure out what kind of learner each of her students is—explicitly. She asks them to write down whether they like to build, to write, or to draw, and from that information she forms the links. She doesn't ignore the basics of language arts, but she encourages her students, too. One boy just couldn't write very well, so she let him type his assignments on the computer or give an occasional oral report.

She loves it when her students are fully engaged. "There's kind of a buzz in the room," she says; they're sitting in small groups, asking lots of questions, talking among themselves, and, eventually, inevitably, walking out of class with a smile.

Beth will tell you that she addresses the assets "in a quiet way." That may be, but her actions shout out to those around her. Ask colleague Trudy Burrus, who says that Beth is "the epitome of the caring adult . . . what a gem; more important, what a natural." Ask any of the Mission Viejo, California, families who've experienced a tragedy; Beth is often the first one to show up with a basket of food and an offer of help. Ask her students, to whom, Beth admits, she gives much more responsibility now than she did before learning about Developmental Assets.

Here's a good example of how Beth has engaged students by making language arts—as well as Developmental Assets—relevant to their lives. As part of a poetry lesson, she asked them to decide if one of the assets in particular had changed for them during the school year. They were to form a verbal diamond, starting with one noun and ending with an opposite noun, with the intervening words bridging the two, followed by an explanation of the diamond. Following is one student's submission:

Lousy
careless disorganized
disliked littered disheveled
miserable vile constructive useful
working rewarding gratifying
vigorous valuable
productive

In the beginning of the year I got lousy grades when I did my homework. I always tried to get it done as fast as possible so then I could go outside and play. I didn't study hard for any tests for school. Then I started to realize that I needed to try harder to do my best and to be productive. I started to spend more time on my homework and I also spent about two hours studying for some of my Social Studies or Science tests. I started to take my work more seriously and then homework became a lot easier to do.

As with other teachers profiled in this book, discovering Developmental Assets affirmed Beth's efforts so far and led her to make some changes in what she's done since. Eight years ago, after attending a presentation about assets, Beth says, "The lightbulb went on. This is what I hope I've been doing all along; now I can do it specifically." She participated in some asset trainings, followed by a training of trainers. Now she's the one making presentations to colleagues, parents, and others.

Beth has also spearheaded trainings of her own. For example, all the bus drivers in her school district have been trained in the asset framework. "They're the first ones to see the kids in the morning; they're the last ones to see them at the end of the day," she says. It makes perfect sense, of course, but not everyone would take the effort to follow through with the idea.

Strange as it may sound, Beth wasn't always aware that she was such an influence on young people—despite the fact that two of her own teachers back in high school, one in accounting and the other in Spanish, inspired her to become a teacher because they made her feel special and gave her positive feedback even when, in her own words, she "messed up." With this new awareness, she's more deliberate about what she does, stopping to listen more often. She's slowed down, because "they're depending on me."

Below are some examples of how Beth relates what she teaches to students:

> She produces a labor-intensive talent show, because, says Beth, "Every child deserves to shine, and this venue may be the place."
> During Open House, her room becomes a Chinese dynasty, each child playing a role.
> She helped create lessons on nonviolence and safety, including in-depth explanations of appropriate responses and quick-reference emergency guides. ("Kids need to know we trust them in emergencies as much as they need to be able to trust us," says Beth.)

If you were a student in Beth's class, wouldn't *you* be interested in performing in a talent show? Wouldn't *you* be interested in playing a role for Open House? Wouldn't *you* want to know what to do in an emergency and know that people—adults—could count on you?

There are other important things that Beth does with her classes, but these are a little different:

> She remembers details about each of her students.
> She spends her time before school and during lunch working with them.
> She often personally finances a student's attendance at a trip or event.

Beth's generosity extends to welcoming young people into her home. In fact, the Groves, parents of four, almost always have someone "extra" living with them—adult family members, a foster son, and, most recently, a senior who was able to graduate from high school only because the Groves took her in after her grandmother/guardian died. (According to Beth's colleague Trudy, "It's like the Holiday Inn, except that you learn to be part of a great family.")

Is all this really necessary in the context of academic achievement? What does remembering details about students or spending extra time with them or paying for their field trips have to do with engaging them in their work?

It has everything to do with it. Engagement transcends curriculum. You're more than an entertainer; your responsibilities don't begin and end with the school day, and your boundaries don't begin and end at the threshold of your classroom.

"Caring" teachers are featured in a separate section, but let this be a foreshadowing of it, because a large part of engagement *is* caring: Engaging students means that you care about them. It means that you've taken the time and energy to figure out just what it is that would, in fact, engage *them*. Students are more interested in a curriculum, more vested in it, when it's about them. We all learn in different ways; that's not a surprise to teachers. Good teachers vary their styles so that sometimes they have students read, other times participate in a play, other times watch a video, other times play a game. The more styles and strategies used, the better the chances of engaging everyone.

But—and this is an important *but*—the more you can relate to your students outside the formal curriculum, the more receptive they'll be to any of those teaching styles, even if it's not their favorite. If students know that you care about them and that you're trying your hardest to interest them in something, then they're more likely to give your efforts a chance. If they think that you're merely trying to entertain everyone as a "strategy" to get them to learn, then they're less likely to stretch for you.

"I want them to know they're coming into a safe place," says Beth, "that we're going to form this bond together." She cares about her students; she tells them about herself, her family, her schooling. She asks about their families. At the beginning of the year, she shares her expectations and has them participate in creating the classroom rules. She says hello to them in line and shakes hands with all of them, asking them a specific question (e.g., what their favorite color is, how many siblings they have).

Often, her former students, now in junior high, come back to say hi. Some students come back regularly. She asks them to tell her sixth graders what to expect, and they're only too happy to oblige. They usually tell students that they appreciate how Beth made them work hard and how she taught them to study. They say that junior high isn't as difficult as they expected.

In the end, such engagement enables Beth to learn a lot from her students, as well. One of them, Brian Hausheer, suggested a new way to do a math problem, so she adopted it and named it after him—the *Hausheer Method*—and wrote a note to his mother informing her of the honor. Later in the year, students would at times say, "Let's use the Hausheer Method."

How can such recognition—by a teacher, by peers, by family—*not* motivate an individual, as well as his or her classmates, to become more engaged in learning? When you engage students, you build assets for everyone involved. As Beth says about all her students, "They bring out the best in me. They make me a better teacher."

> > >

engaging teachers involve students' peers, families, and community. It sounds simple enough to relate curricular activities to students' lives, but it's not done nearly often enough. Students' lives involve their friends, classmates, school adults, neighbors, and family members— all potential teaching assistants. Students' lives involve the places they go to eat, to buy clothes, and to be entertained—all potential surrogate classrooms. Engaging teachers break the boundaries of the classroom; they bring the students' world inside even as they're pushing the curriculum outside.

tom kidd

> GRADES 6, 7, AND 8
> DE LONG MIDDLE SCHOOL, EAU CLAIRE, WI

"If it doesn't make a difference in the quality of their life every day, then I don't teach it." That's Tom Kidd's simple approach to engaging his students. Granted, Tom teaches health, and it's a lot easier to make sex and drugs meaningful to students than, say, the state capitals, but the philosophy holds. He makes what he teaches relevant, so his students are engaged. And it shows.

During a visit to DeLong Middle School in Eau Claire, the wife of the governor of Wisconsin asked students what they were proudest of. One girl said that she was proud of how diverse the school was and how people of different religions and cultures got along so well. When asked how that happened, the girl replied that the teachers teach them that and model those behaviors.

Tom is one of the teachers the girl was undoubtedly thinking of. Although he believes he's been building Developmental Assets all during his 27 years of teaching, Tom began doing it explicitly in the 1998–1999 school year. He teaches a nine-week health course at DeLong, and it's easy to see that he teaches as well as models through highly interactive activities and by emphasizing engagement with the greater community. Every day, a lesson addresses at least one of the assets. He now begins his sixth- and seventh-grade classes in the following way each year:

He presents three wrapped gifts next to a "Win me" sign. Students write their names on slips of paper and throw them into a box. Tom then draws a slip of paper from the box that he's already put in himself; the slip of paper says "Everyone." Tom tells his class, "What's in these gift boxes is worth more than a million dollars: It's health, happiness, and success." He says that the secrets to achieving those gifts are Developmental Assets.

He gives students an asset checklist and a copy for their parents to take and compare. He sends home a letter to parents introducing Developmental Assets that includes the checklist and a Developing My Assets plan: "Please discuss with [your child] how you plan to maintain the assets they have while you help them get some more of their assets met." The plan refers to a specific asset and two statements, one for the student ("My plan is to develop the above asset in my life by . . .") and the other for the parents ("Our plan is to develop the above asset in _____'s life by . . .").

How do the parents respond? According to Tom, "Their eyes get big, their mouth drops open, and it's 'Whoa, this is good.'" The assets strike home on two levels, he says: First, they affirm the good things parents are already doing. And second, "They're always looking for something that works." For those students whose parents don't have time to complete the checklist and discuss it, Tom has students choose another significant adult in their lives—a neighbor, a staff member—to review the checklist with. And, since almost a quarter of his students' families are Asian, he's having the checklist and other materials translated into other languages, such as Hmong. Tom solicits feedback on the plans from students and their parents throughout the nine-week unit.

Tom estimates that 85 percent of his activities are hands-on or interactive. For example, when he wants students to learn about the physical effects of smoking, he has them pinch their noses and then stand and sit 10 times quickly, so their breathing becomes labored. Then he tells them, "This is what it feels like to have a condition called emphysema." He's continually looking for new ideas—from colleagues, from students, from television—to use in his teaching.

One idea that's always in use: Tom writes a description of each asset on colored neon card stock and displays them in his classroom every day. He ties in a Developmental Asset to every lesson. In one of his activities, students connect assets to facts; for example, "Fact: Family closeness is good for you!" He also includes a description and a citation (e.g., *Journal of Early Adolescence*).

But what Tom does most effectively is expand the classroom—to the school community and outward to the larger community. His goal is for his students to start conversations with families, friends, and others about health-related subjects. He works diligently to have his students go out to the neighborhood and to bring the neighborhood into the classroom. Here are a few examples:

> Tom's Community Asset Building Council, comprising youth representatives from eight local schools, trains community organizations—PTAs, law enforcement, social service groups—in Developmental Assets. The training includes personal plans and team plans.

> Tom sends a list with explanations of the assets to Eau Claire's maternity wards and hospitals. He's also considering sending postcards six months later to remind new parents about building assets.

> His students present the person chosen as Asset Builder of the Month by the Community Asset Building Council with a certificate of appreciation, and place an article in the Community section of their local newspaper, the *Leader-Telegram*.

> He has submitted 40 "Building Up Kids" pages—one for each asset—to the parenting section of the newspaper, with suggestions for parents, schools, and the community.

> He has a Jar of Assets, from which his students periodically choose slips of paper with various assets written on them. If

they draw one of the external assets, they're obligated to build that asset in someone else's life. If they draw one of the internal assets, they're obligated to work on that asset themselves.

> Throughout the year, he asks his students to perform at least 10 hours of service with an adult from the school or greater community.

The school community is important to Tom. His students write morning announcements to be broadcast over the school intercom. Each announcement introduces a Developmental Asset, states why it's important to the speaker, and suggests how to strengthen the asset. For example, a suggestion for Caring School Climate might be "Thank a teacher, an administrator, a cook, or a custodian today for providing a caring environment here at DeLong." And a suggestion for Creative Activities might be "Go an extra 30 minutes tonight when practicing your instrument, playing sports, or rehearsing for a variety show."

Along with his colleagues, Tom facilitates Cooperating for Change groups—students who meet once a week for 10 weeks during study time. The groups address topics of direct relevance to students—how to make friends, how to have stronger relationships with family members, how to cope if your family is in upheaval, how to respond to a loss—all tied in to the building of assets. Each group has two adult facilitators and about a dozen students. All the students are volunteers, and Tom says that they represent a spectrum of the school community.

While this may sound like a good idea, not everyone at school originally thought so. DeLong Principal Deb Hansen remembers that when Tom was first hired and proposed the Cooperating for Change groups, the Guidance Department was surprised that someone other than a counselor wanted to facilitate the group. Tom neither fought nor gave up. He researched the idea, met with everyone concerned, and proposed a pilot program. He offered ways that counselors could help and eventually brought everyone together to initiate the program. Currently, 65 percent of the teachers at DeLong Middle School have been trained to facilitate the groups. "He took his time and did his homework," says

Hansen, "and had the patience to wait to bring everyone else along with him. I think he does that with kids, too." She adds that if a topic is too difficult or sophisticated for students, he'll help them get to the needed level so they're not intimidated or embarrassed—an important thing to remember when students are learning new skills.

For Tom, who always believed that education—and, for that matter, prevention—extended well beyond the classroom, the assets "solidified what I do in prevention. I like to see the kids change and grow with the more knowledge that they have and the more life skills that are given to them. . . . Educating children is a priceless gift. It's critical to our society, critical to their lives." By engaging students in ideas and skills, Tom is opening up the classroom to his students' entire world.

Take life skills. What Tom means by life skills are strategies, for example, to resist peer pressure and to use self-control. These skills square nicely with assets such as Resistance Skills and Peaceful Conflict Resolution, but they also have an impact on assets such as Interpersonal Competence, Personal Power, and Positive View of Personal Future. And Tom makes sure that students do more than memorize the skills; he wants them to use them.

Tom's passion for helping young people engage in healthy behaviors is apparent to others. Bette Wahl belongs to a community-based group called the Eau Claire Coalition for Youth (she's in the Special Services Bureau of the Police Department, "on the prevention end of things") and has worked with Tom since 1998 on the Community Asset Building Council. She doesn't remember the exact circumstances of meeting him, but, she says,

> I know I was immediately impressed with his charisma and felt like I had always known him. You know by instinct that this person has a passion for kids and the kids love Tom. I've been in his classroom after school and kids are constantly dropping by to say hi, for advice and support, or just to be near someone who cares about them.

Tom didn't always have this level of passion, knowledge, and expertise, certainly not the first few years he taught. It was when he finally felt comfortable teaching that it became his passion. It develops, he says, over time. "A lot of teachers quit before they develop it. We need teachers who truly care about the whole child."

It is this caring, in part, that stimulates the desire to be engaging. Tom has found *how* to engage students because he cares about them. It's central to the work of all the teachers in this book; it's as if they can teach no other way.

Tom once had a student who was suffering from attention deficit disorder as well as some emotional problems. The boy wasn't at school a lot, and when he was, it was hard to get through to him. Trying to connect was a constant struggle, Tom says, but he persisted. He sat the boy down after school and got him to commit to come to class. He calls his strategy a "carefrontation"—approaching someone directly about an important issue in a caring way. This is as much an attitude as a skill; it means, essentially, that in order to engage the student, the goal is to help, not to judge. Eventually, the boy made some better decisions and became involved with a different crowd. He graduated from high school, attended technical college, and got married. Later, he thanked Tom for interceding in his life, for caring about him, and for giving him useful skills. Tom teaches a "carefrontation" skill to all his students now, so they can approach relatives, friends, and others they care about.

Tom makes it sound simple. But what happens if students don't develop the Developmental Asset they're responsible for? What happens if despite your best efforts, despite your reaching out to all parts of their lives, they don't build their assets, don't learn the skills?

Tom doesn't acknowledge failures, for two reasons. The first is that he has a healthy sense of his and his students' responsibilities. For example, if students don't fulfill an assignment of any kind, he says, "I offer them the opportunity to make it up. If they still choose not to do it, I've done the best I can." Remember, Tom teaches Developmental Assets in each of three grades—sixth, seventh, and eighth—so he has three yearlong chances with each student. (Not only that, but many of the high school teachers in Eau Claire intentionally build assets, too.)

The second reason he doesn't acknowledge failures is one that all teachers might take to heart: You never know when you've made the positive impact you're striving for. As Tom says, "They may get all this information and skills [now, but] two years down the road it starts clicking." The truth is, teachers often make positive differences and don't know it, either because it hasn't yet "clicked" with the student or because it has and the student hasn't acknowledged or shared it. When you meaningfully engage students, you're increasing the chances that the impact you have won't dissipate as the students leave the school. "If they have fun while they're learning," as Tom says about his students, "it'll last forever."

> > >

engaging teachers allow students to be themselves. Engaging teachers—good teachers—know what's important. Much as trusting teachers learn to give up control, engaging teachers learn to allow students to be themselves. When students are chastised for having different opinions, when students are teased for the way they're dressed, when students are compelled to follow a lesson plan exactly the way it's developed, the teacher is being *dis*engaging. Think of it this way: It's not you versus the students in an attempt to teach them what they don't want to learn. It's you *and* the students with a common goal of transferring knowledge. They're your allies; shouldn't you make them as comfortable as possible while still challenging them to do their best?

andrea godfrey brown

> **GRADES 11 AND 12**
> **PARKWAY SOUTH HIGH SCHOOL, MANCHESTER, MO**

Persevering despite the barriers is what engaging students in learning is all about for Andrea Godfrey Brown. "I'm really stubborn, and I don't give up." The student that she can't reach? "That's the kid I'll be thinking about driving home."

But what's her strategy? "Some of it is who I am and some of it is what I do," sums up Andie fittingly. She considers herself a continual, lifelong learner, and students pick up on that immediately. "Very early on," she says, "I try to let them see me really excited about learning *with* them." And because she herself can be easily engaged by something different, something unusual, she's less apt to be judgmental: A student may say something seemingly out of context and off track, and while other teachers might be dismissive or want to redirect the conversation, Andie might genuinely say, "Oh, I have never thought of it like that!"

Andie wasn't always this way as a teacher, however. The epiphany came for her several years ago. She was teaching as many teachers do: standing up in front of the classroom, controlling the discussions, feeding students information and hoping they'd digest it. But her students weren't responding to what she was asking them to do, and they were resisting what she was *telling* them to do. In one memorable moment, Andie realized here was another way to approach teaching and engage her students: Rather than simply trying to instill knowledge, she could attempt instead to facilitate their learning. And it was at that moment that, subconsciously, she began to build Developmental Assets intentionally with her students. "I've begun to see it more as a partnership," she says about her current relationship with her students. "When they feel that you're a partner, they don't fight you anymore."

They certainly don't fight *her* anymore. As Andie's principal, Gary Mazzola, says, "Andie really understands how to build relationships with her kids; you'll have to search long and hard to find a teacher more popular with his or her students. . . . Kids respect Andie because she understands the difference between power and influence."

There are chairs in Andie's classroom, but there's also a couch and pillows scattered throughout the room. One student even likes to lie on the floor; Andie has no problem with that. In this particular language arts class, "Grisham's Novels," students are discussing John Grisham's *The Street Lawyer.* They've just finished reading the novel, and typically she would take them all out for breakfast. A scheduling conflict, however, prompts her to bring in pastries, sausages, and drinks instead. Students take turns microwaving the sausages and handing out the rest of the food.

Andie plans to have two groups alternate discussions with quiet work. One student demurs, however, and suggests that instead they have an all-class discussion. Andie wavers and decides to put it to a vote. The class votes for the larger-group discussion. Andie asks one girl—who'd said that the large group sometimes intimidated her—if she is okay with that, and the girl says yes.

The discussion ostensibly focuses on the novel—a prosperous, successful lawyer's attempt to live among, understand, and advocate for the homeless—but Andie extrapolates it to other issues: whether one person can make a difference in others' lives, whether students give to charity, how close students' families are to being poor, the extent to which welfare is beneficial, what it means to walk away from wealth in order to do good for society. Everyone participates, including the girl who'd earlier voiced that sometimes she feels intimidated.

The students are highly engaged and assets abound. At the top, of course, is Reading for Pleasure, but there's also School Engagement, Honesty, and Personal Power. As Ivan, a senior, puts it, they can talk about anything in class, and he and others have gained confidence as a result. Barb, a parent whose three children have all been taught by Andie, says that Andie "allows them to be who they are." Barb's husband, Tim, thinks that there are never wrong answers in Andie's class, merely different ways of thinking about things. Their son, Mike, participates in Cadet Teaching, which means that he actually leads some of the class discussions with his peers.

Mike is, in some ways, a classic Andie Brown story. According to Andie, he was comfortable with who he was, but he was a misfit at school. Mike figured he was competent enough in music and writing, but he didn't have confidence in his ability to succeed academically. And while his appearance didn't inspire confidence from some, it didn't bother Andie at all. A student in her class on Kurt Vonnegut, he'd come in wearing a black trench coat, with his fingernails painted and hair dyed.

With a large infusion of Andie's trust, Mike became a leader in the class. She found Mike had no problems carrying on discussions with his fellow students. It was not unusual for him to invite everyone over to his house to work on a project. To further engage him, she advocated strongly for him to become a "Cadet Teacher." He flourished.

At one point, Andie was raving to Mike's father about how wonderful he was, and Tim choked up as he acknowledged that Mike was indeed gifted. "If I did anything for Mike," says Andie, "it was to show him he had some specialness in a school setting." Barb says that had Andie not been there, Mike probably would have dropped out.

It's fortunate for Mike and the other students that Andie found her way to a career in education. Andie wasn't always a teacher. She was a paralegal assistant for three years, until she took on a case that made her question her ethics. She decided that she didn't like what she was doing and left law. She began tutoring children and then taught in a small private school. She became a counselor and landed a job at Parkway South High School, a larger school with 2,000 students in grades 9 through 12.

When she first learned of Developmental Assets about eight years ago, Andie's youngest son was in middle school. "I wanted to make sure that my kid had the assets that I could help build as a parent," she says. But then she thought about what she could do to build assets as a teacher. "For some people," she says, "assets might be a fad. . . . For me, this makes both emotional sense and intellectual sense. It feels right, and it has been backed up by unbelievably intensive research."

Now she writes her curricula—such as the courses on Grisham and Vonnegut—with the idea of building Developmental Assets in mind. Here are the guidelines, for example, that help her engage everyone in building the Reading for Pleasure asset in her classes:

1. Teach something both the students and the teachers like.
2. Listen to students and incorporate their ideas into the next part of the teacher's work.

3. Help students deal with and discuss books as adults do, and apply the books' ideas to current social issues.
4. Drive the discussions through a student-led approach.
5. Evaluate differently than in traditional core courses.
6. Use the "student as worker, teacher as coach" philosophy.
7. Teach students how to take the risk of creating diverse groups to accomplish tasks.
8. Make personal connections to the reading.

Andie strongly believes that building Developmental Assets needs to be intentional. She doesn't find that difficult to do, nor does she find it difficult to create and plan assessments while meeting school and state standards. In fact, she says, ever since she started intentionally building assets, she rarely has any discipline problems, so the time she spends on building relationships to engage students is more than worth it. And she's able to engage students by letting them be themselves.

As a result, the students experience positive relationships and enjoy school, which in turn leads to achievement. What's important to Andie is that her students discover that they're really good at something—and she especially loves working with young people others have given up on. "They can write," she insists. "They can write important things."

Andie's currently working with a very quiet girl who missed most of her sophomore year because of eating disorders. Andie convinced her to write a "My Turn" essay describing her struggles, and then encouraged her to edit the essay and enter it into a contest. Not only did this student give voice to her life experiences, but she was also able to articulate them in a way that read beautifully. The whole process "was one of those breakthrough moments for this young woman," says Andie proudly. The girl turned what she perceived to be a weakness into a strength.

Other students aren't as easy to help. "Kids today have lives that are really different than what I think adults wish were true," says Andie. She cites students who are in a lot of trouble without even being aware of it, and she admits to not knowing what to say sometimes to young people who, for example, have been having casual sex or using heroin since seventh grade. But with all that, there's been only one student whom she tried to remove from her class.

This boy said something hateful to her in front of the rest of the students. She was stunned and barely responded. To Andie, it seemed as if she and the boy could never connect; she wasn't even sure she wanted to. She called the boy's parents to say that she didn't think she could teach him, and she recommended that he transfer to another class. It turned out, however, that he was unable to transfer, and he remained in her class. For weeks, they didn't speak to each other—an uneasy truce. Near the end of the course, he took a risk and wrote something autobiographical for an assignment—something that made Andie understand a little more why he was so angry, why he'd lashed out at her. They didn't wind up being the best of friends, but at least she identified a rationale for his behavior.

Even the very best teachers—and Andie Brown is one of the very best teachers—meet hurdles that they can't get over, just as you do. You may extend yourself as much as you can, you may do everything you're supposed to do and more, but you still may not reach every student. That's not a failure; that's life. And it points out something that bears remembering: Just as you have a responsibility to engage students, students have a responsibility to be receptive. If despite all your efforts, a student is reluctant to participate in schoolwork, then that's when you have to say to yourself, "I've done my best, I'll continue to do my best, but I can't take all the responsibility here for the outcome."

Clearly Andie is doing her best. One of her student's comments speaks to this very issue of individual responsibility—and achievement—attained because of Andie's teaching: "I think that taking this class made me a better writer and person. I think this class taught me some needed responsibility that I wouldn't have gotten elsewhere in my senior year."

Similar engagement and achievement were attained recently by her honors juniors studying a unit on the war in Vietnam. Andie bused the students to the Jefferson Barracks National Cemetery, where they sat quietly reading and looking out at the thousands of veterans' gravestones. The initial idea to go to the cemetery, explains Andie, "was an attempt to do something real—not just read about how many died in such-and-such war, but really look at and reflect about the gravestones in front of us."

The students ended up doing much more than just reflect on their visit. When they returned to school, the students began raising money to build a local monument honoring veterans. They wrote letters, conducted fund-raisers, and worked on a design. They made a presentation to the local Veterans of Foreign Wars chapter and secured a donation of $1,000. (They raised another $2,500 through donations and ticket sales to the student talent show they helped organize.)

The students negotiated with the stonecutter, who made the monument. The students held a ceremony to thank the contributors and unveil the statue. It stands today in the school parking lot—a black marble base, capped with a bronze American eagle, inscribed "Freedom is not free."

Earlier in the year, these same students were given the opportunity to solve real-life problems of producing a play. Says Andie, "Instead of just reading *The Crucible*, I challenged them to put on a production and invite other junior classes to watch it. Their success or failure would be public. They struggled, mightily at times, and persevered. These were kids who were empowered."

Years from now, when these students reflect on their high school days, you can imagine what will stand out most of all for them. Think of all the Developmental Assets at work in both these projects, and others. Think of all the experience they gained.

But it's not only engaging the students in positive and memorable learning experiences that matters; it's also the relationships behind those experiences. "I care what they think," says Andie about her students. "I really try to communicate with them very early on." And the students get that. As one tells her, "I almost don't consider you my teacher. It's more like a friendship."

That's critical for Andie—to be real, to be a friend. She remembers her little sister, at seven years old, bursting into tears after seeing her teacher in the grocery store because she'd thought that the teacher lived at school. Andie doesn't ever want her students to think that she lives at the school, that she's not a normal person.

Here's what engaging students in learning and in building assets comes down to for Andie: She was "bad" in high school, always getting into trouble, to the extent that she was sent away to a boarding school. There she was fortunate to have a principal, Art Schulz, who believed in her, who didn't give up on her. At one point, she wanted to work on a project that involved writing poetry with young people who were incarcerated. The faculty didn't want anything to do with it. Principal Schulz overrode their concerns. "I'm going to let you do this," he told Andie, who remembers this vividly, "because you're on the 4-F system: the Freedom to Fall Flat on your Face. Why don't you prove them wrong?" He gave her a chance—to be herself and to find herself—the same chance she gives students such as Mike.

Andie hears Art Schulz in her head sometimes. "Thank God he did not give up on me," she says. "I want to carry that on."

asset-building
teachers

> *I'm there to support them and to help them learn about themselves.*

MARK HENDRIX

all the teachers profiled in this book focus on academic achievement. Particularly in these days of accountability and assessment, of the federal No Child Left Behind Act and State Department of Education Standards for Achievement, of activist parents and hard-pressed administrators, teachers are acutely aware that they need to teach their subject matter and teach it well. The question, then, is this: How does building Developmental Assets help with the primary mandate of teaching the school's curriculum?

Research suggests that having increased levels of the assets has a significant impact on students' academic performance—for students of all races, ethnicities, and socioeconomic backgrounds. In fact, the assets appear to have as much, if not more, influence on student achievement *as other demographic factors and school reform strategies.*[2] *And even in the day-to-day routine of teaching, we know from teachers such as Susan Cressey and Andie Brown that assets can be seamlessly woven into whatever is being taught, and that the incorporation of Developmental Assets can enhance the curriculum and student teaching.*

In this section, you'll read about four teachers who not only have infused asset building into how they teach, but also have designed their curricula to include courses that teach students about Developmental Assets. Jenny Goldberg-McDonnell teaches in a Colorado middle school, Sean Yeager in an Idaho middle school, Sandy Eggleston in a New York elementary school, and Mark Hendrix in a California high school. All of them developed and teach courses specifically about Developmental Assets because of their ability to make the case that assets are a boon to academic achievement, and that asset building is done best when it's done for, with, and by students.

Whatever subject you teach, in whatever grade you teach, think about what these teachers are doing and how you might do something similar. Ask yourself: "How can I adapt my curriculum to make it more consistent with asset building? How can I blend the intentional building of Developmental Assets with the standards I'm required to meet? How can I convince others that students will benefit from such a blend of assets and academics? How can I incorporate the use of the Developmental Assets framework into the school and greater community so that it's operational and sustainable?"

> > >

[2] Scales, Peter C., & Roehlkepartain, Eugene C. (2003). Boosting student achievement: New research on the power of developmental assets. *Search Institute Insights & Evidence, 1*(1), 1–10.

asset-building teachers incorporate Developmental Assets into the school curriculum. The Developmental Assets framework gives good teachers a new language to describe what they've already been doing. Nowhere is this truer than in school curricula. Assets such as Creative Activities, Homework, and Reading for Pleasure may be natural by-products of teaching, but asset-building teachers will also incorporate some of the assets that may require a little more effort to build and that have correlations to achievement, such as Service to Others, Bonding to School, Planning and Decision Making, and Personal Power. Asset-building teachers know that they can incorporate assets not only in *how* they teach but also in *what* they teach.

jenny goldberg-mcdonnell

> GRADES 6, 7, AND 8
> KEPNER MIDDLE SCHOOL, DENVER, CO

When teachers at Kepner Middle School have asked Jenny Goldberg-McDonnell why students act differently for her than for them, the answer is easy. Says Jenny, "The more you care about your students . . . the more they're going to want to give back to you. If you can't build relationships, the test scores mean nothing."

For Jenny, incorporating the Developmental Assets, which are built through strong adult-youth relationships, into Kepner's school community has made a tremendous difference. "It's part of their daily lives," she says, echoing what so many other educators in this book have said. "It's a culture more than a curriculum."

And because the Developmental Assets framework is more of a philosophy than a program, it's sufficiently flexible to be interwoven into almost everything. Incorporating assets and asset building into the school curriculum can thus run the gamut from adding asset-building activities to programs in language arts, math, science, health, and other areas of study, all the way to administering asset courses that help students see how they can build the assets in their own lives and in the lives of their peers.

Using positive, encouraging language all day in her efforts to build relationships with her students, Jenny shows "them several assets every day in the fact of being involved with them. I notice when they're here, when they're gone, when their attitude is different, how their learning styles differ."

Jenny is successful at it, as shown by the fact that many students don't even want to go home after school. "They know [school is] a place that they're cared about." There's a long waiting list to get into Kepner Middle School; something must be working.

Jenny's commitment to good teaching doesn't stem from a lifelong dream of being an educator. When she first left college, she planned to open a child-care center, but soon became interested in drama. Next followed a career in sales, and after *that*, she managed a clothing store. Eventually, however, she decided that she "wanted to do something worthwhile" and returned to her original degree in order to teach. (She recently received her M.A. in curriculum and instruction.) She got a substitute-teaching job at Denver's Lincoln High School and then transferred to Kepner Middle School.

After attending an Assets for Colorado Youth "Expect Success" training workshop, Jenny thought that the assets "made common sense." With the active encouragement of her principal, she wrote the curriculum for a leadership class called "Assets in Action." The class is an elective—one 45-minute period a day for each grade. She now teaches the class and heads the school's Assets Team, which includes the principal, assistant principal, school psychologist, and several office staff, teachers, and parents.

During the assets class, students address the "asset of the day," writing about what the asset means to them. Students choose partners and write skits based on specific Developmental Assets—say, Integrity, in which one student might try to get another to skip class. The course also involves participation in community service projects, including coordinating a food drive for poor families in the neighborhood. The students even publish a guide to the assets for parents as well as a school newspaper that includes an asset checklist.

Jenny also teaches a gifted/talented class. In this class, students choose from a list of 35 projects to work on. Some students have created calendars that incorporate the assets. Other students have been given "money" to plan a vacation for a fictitious family of four to a country they'll soon be studying. They're asked to use the Internet and other sources to gather their research. One student developed a cooking show, with all the other students helping her to bake a cake. Another student wrote a book that illustrates how to play the keyboard.

As part of the Developmental Assets approach, students are required to read at least 30 minutes every day, as well as interact with their parents. For their part, parents sign a contract that encourages them to be involved and to ask their children four questions:

1. "What did you learn today?"
2. "What's your homework?"
3. "What's in your planner?"
4. "What did you read?"

This type of contract builds the asset of Parent Involvement in Schooling and can be woven into virtually any subject. The idea—extending the learning activities to parents—is valid regardless of the subject.

That's not to say that this particular component is always successful. Many of the students' home situations are complex—both parents are working, younger siblings have higher needs, and so on. Jenny tries to make all of her phone contacts with parents positive, and she does what she can to help parents. "We don't have to see their faces to know they're involved," she says.

One involved parent, Rae Ann, the mother of one of Jenny's eighth-grade students, notes the following about Jenny:

I've asked for help with certain situations and she has always responded to me and tried to help in any way that she can. She has talked to my son to try and help him succeed in his goal to move on to high school. She's helped me by keeping in touch with me and letting me know my son's progress and his "back falls" within her class, and his other classes as well. . . . She has given me strength to continue to push my child and thanks to her words, "Don't give up on him," I hear them every day, and it helps me to push my son harder to do his very best! I am a single mom and just having that support helps out a great deal!

As evidenced by this testimonial, it's no secret why students "behave" for Jenny, or why she's even gotten requests to talk to some of her former students, who are now with other teachers.

It was actually Principal Debbie Lanman who first introduced the idea of using the Developmental Assets framework in a leadership course, but she's quick to give credit to Jenny for maintaining the assets as a focus in the school. Debbie likes the assets because "it's a framework for helping students be responsible for themselves." And as Jenny notes, "I revel in [giving up control to students]. If you don't, then you'll never really know the level of their potential."

Debbie points out the impact students have on the process of asset building itself. During staff meetings to include the asset language throughout the school, students read their compositions about assets. "It's very moving," she says. "That is very powerful, when teachers can see that [the asset framework is] supporting students and affecting their lives. That's when it becomes very basic for teachers, not something extra to do but something necessary."

As with all the teachers in this book, there are interesting—even touching—success stories. There was a girl with whom Jenny had "quite a confrontation, really a struggle" on the very first day of class. The student didn't want to participate in the asset activities, had a "large attitude problem," and was struggling with taking part in the class at all. Jenny took the girl out in the hall for a conversation, making two important points: First, the girl's behavior was unacceptable. And second, she cared about her. In one brief talk, Jenny tried to build the assets of Caring School Climate, School Boundaries, and High Expectations.

The next week brought a few changes, with the girl herself showing asset-building behavior. Jenny asked the girl to help her with a few things, and the girl got a sense of contributing to the classroom. Jenny called the girl's mother to give her some positive feedback. "After that," says Jenny, "it was a phenomenal change." The girl began paying attention, helping, even becoming the "September Star of the Month." She still has lapses—she has power struggles with other teachers and pushes them to their limit—but Jenny says, "I'm not letting her get me there." If the girl is having a bad day, Jenny checks in with her, asks her if she's okay, and usually things get better.

When Jenny is teaching—whether the subject is assets, aardvarks, or artichokes—she firmly believes that relationships are at the core of *good* teaching. The focus on Developmental Assets supports that idea, as well as giving guidance to its specifics: "Building relationships is imperative, not an extra. It can't be something that's left out." She calls herself a pragmatist—a student-centered, hands-on pragmatist. "Some teachers don't enjoy the process," she says. "But you get what you give. [I teach this way because] I want to enjoy what I'm doing—forever. I don't want to be burned out next year."

> > >

asset-building teachers incorporate asset building into the school environment. Establishing a norm for building assets is like establishing a norm for discouraging violence, or resisting drugs, or supporting classmates; it depends on a critical mass of people adhering to positive attitudes and taking positive actions. The Developmental Assets framework needs to be operationalized throughout the school environment for individual students to gain the most benefit from asset building. All the Positive-Values assets—Caring, Equality and Social Justice,

Integrity, Honesty, Responsibility, and Restraint—are strengthened when reinforced by influential peers. So are the Commitment-to-Learning assets and many of the others. Asset-building teachers seek to integrate the framework wherever they can, and that makes it easier for the whole school community to talk about and coordinate efforts so that everyone's giving—and getting—consistent messages.

sean yeager

> GRADES 7 AND 8
> SOUTH MIDDLE SCHOOL, NAMPA, ID

At age 28, in western Montana, Sean Yeager told his pregnant wife that he couldn't sell office supplies anymore. He liked people, but he couldn't "close": If someone wasn't interested in buying something, Sean didn't want to pressure the person to do so.

His wife, Rachelle, asked him what he liked to do. "Well," said Sean, "I've always liked coaching." "Well, then . . . ," said Rachelle. Sean returned to school, acquired his teaching credentials, and is now teaching a course in Developmental Assets for seventh- and eighth-grade students at South Middle School, Nampa, Idaho.

In the years since learning about assets, Sean has taught a variety of classes—health, P.E.—all with different names, but all based in the asset framework. Sean believes that he can fit the assets into virtually anything he teaches. In his current class, which is a semester long, each asset category constitutes a unit, beginning with Commitment to Learning. "I'm teaching kids at school," says Sean, "what many kids used to learn at home."

Here's a closer look at Sean's asset-building course:

> **Weeks 1, 2, 3, and 4: Commitment to Learning**—taking notes, setting goals, managing time

> **Weeks 5 and 6: Social Competencies**—making positive choices, building relationships, resolving conflicts, responding to peer pressure, appreciating other cultures, becoming aware of those with disabilities
> **Weeks 7 and 8: Support** (including Family, Friends, and Community)—understanding the importance of relationships with adults
> **Weeks 9 and 10: Empowerment** (including Service, Safety, and Family Boundaries)—examining local and national organizations that provide supportive environments, learning about the benefits of community service
> **Weeks 11 and 12: Constructive Use of Time**—experiencing opportunities for growth through creative activities, youth programs, and time at home
> **Weeks 13 and 14: Positive Identity**—building self-esteem
> **Weeks 15 and 16: Boundaries and Expectations**—sharing what adults at school and home expect from students, as well as what students expect from adults at school and home
> **Weeks 17 and 18: Positive Values**—strengthening students' sense of their own power, purpose, worth, and promise

The course has been an astounding success—for both Sean and the students. He's noticed some pronounced changes in his students, and he's not alone: Parents tell Sean that their children's study habits have improved since they began his class. "It's been an amazing experience," he says. "I love it there. And I know that they love coming to my class."

Part of this enjoyment comes from the strategies Sean uses in implementing the Developmental Assets framework in and out of the classroom. For example, in classroom discipline, he focuses on taking away rewards instead of punishing. If students are talking during class, he writes their names on the board rather than stopping the class; that's a warning. If they do something else objectionable during that period, they get a check by their name and a 15-minute lunch detention. Respect is key. He tells them, "I'll do my best not to talk down to you, but you have to treat me with the same respect. If you act like a kid, then I'm going to treat you like a kid." It seems to be working. "When you get to know the students," he says, "you know what's most effective for each one."

Recently, Sean's class was discussing consequences: If you make a mistake, the important thing is to learn from it and not repeat it. A student stood up and announced that he wanted to share something. He said that he and a friend had been caught drinking on school grounds. He'd thought that it was "the thing to do" and hadn't considered the consequences. The boy then talked about what could have happened, such as getting into a car accident. He said that he'd gotten suspended, but that he felt lucky because it could have been much worse.

The class is a microcosm of the real world—and that's not an accident. "Teaching," says Sean, "is all about finding connections, presenting something in a way they can relate to." For an activity about peer pressure, students interviewed their parents about the pressures they had to confront when they were young. For an activity about safety, students drew a picture of the school and colored areas based on how safe they felt there.

When you include building assets in your classroom teaching, the effects aren't bounded by the classroom; they extend into the broader school environment. Teachers point out that the lessons learned by focusing on the asset framework—taking responsibility, being considerate, resolving conflicts peacefully—are repeatedly validated in students' lives outside the class.

Sean's experiences with his own students' lives are typical in this regard. Since he also coaches boys' and girls' basketball at South Middle School, he gets to present consistent asset-building messages in a variety of situations. For Sean, sports is an all-encompassing metaphor for life. "I love the idea," he says, "of taking sports and comparing it with real life. We're all working toward a common goal. We're all parts of an engine, and we all have to work together to get the car to move. You're all working together and relying on each other."

Sean emphasizes to his students the importance of responding moderately to different situations: Don't get too excited when things are going well; don't give up when things are going poorly. He wants his 7-year-old to learn how to win—and lose—gracefully. "If we coddle them and don't let them experience [difficulties]," says Sean, "then when real life hits, they're going to have to deal with it somehow."

This all may sound like a lot of work, but, like most of the teachers in this book, Sean doesn't consider it quite work. He loves walking down the hall, talking with students. "It's not just the classes," he says. "It's the time in between."

And with Sean, there's plenty of time in between. After the bell, he talks to his students, "levels with them," asks them, for example, what he can do to get them to turn in their homework. In the gym, however, he can't take away participation because some students don't like to participate—to do exercises, for example. So he's taken to calling students' parents, and that seems to be working. He gets the parents' support, and the student shapes up.

Of course, there are moments when a teacher forgets to take an asset-building approach to a sensitive situation. During one P.E. session, at the beginning of class when Sean was doing some administrative chores with his educational assistant, he saw a boy and girl wrestling with each other. It wasn't playful wrestling, either; the girl was trying to bite the boy's hand.

Sean said, "Stop!" and the angry girl bit the boy anyway. He immediately escorted her to the dean's office. On the way to the office, however, the girl asserted that the boy had been trying to pull her pants down. Sean felt terrible; in the class, he hadn't been willing to hear what she had to say.

He returned with her to the class in order to get the boy, but the boy refused to come along. Sean, who has always prided himself in not letting his emotions get the better of him, raised his voice and said, "You will come with me right now." The boy, all eyes upon him, still refused. Sean eventually brought the girl to the office and got security staff to bring the boy in. He considers the incident a failure on his part because he didn't set a good example—by listening before acting, by thinking before raising his voice—and he thinks that the nature of the class changed as a result.

Still, the successes are numerous. Teachers in South Middle School have "advisory classes," in which students read during the first half hour and participate in a group activity during the second half hour. Soon after Sean's class had been discussing the topic of persuasion, the wood-shop teacher told Sean about the success of some of the girls in his advisory class (who are also in Sean's class). The advisory class had discussed picking up trash as their group project, but only five voted in favor of it. The girls then made statements to the class in order to persuade the rest of the students to pick up trash. They did it in the format that Sean's class had discussed; as a result, 75 percent of the class was persuaded to vote yes.

That's the kind of multiplier effect that can happen when the Developmental Assets framework is infused beyond a single classroom into the larger school environment. People set examples for others, who in turn set examples for still others. Each time, the behaviors are reinforced.

Whether it's knowing that the assets are being built or hearing about the successes of his students, Sean feels justly rewarded. "What we get in return," he says, "the rewards we have, feeling good about ourselves, making a positive impact on kids—you can't put a dollar sign on that. My alarm clock goes off, I don't dread a thing. I'm fired up. I'm excited."

> > >

asset-building teachers incorporate Developmental Assets into the community environment. After incorporating the Developmental Assets framework into the school environment, the next logical step is incorporating it into the community environment. When you have civic officials, business representatives, and care providers—in addition to parents and young people—all aware of the importance of building assets, then each individual student is more likely to get support. Think of the assets of Caring Neighborhood, Safety, Adult Role Models, and Youth Programs, and then consider which groups of people in your community are best fitted to help build those assets.

sandy eggleston

> GRADE 1
> PINE BROOK ELEMENTARY SCHOOL, GREECE, NY

Sandy Eggleston infuses assets into everything—her personal behavior, her classroom, her plans for curriculum, her relationships with parents, the entire school—and beyond. In fact, her influence has pervaded not only Pine Brook Elementary School but also the community of Greece, New York. Greece has the seventh-largest school district in the state.

And she regards it all as just "something you do every day." That's if an example of "something you do every day" is sewing and stuffing more than 24 pillows that classrooms created to donate to local agencies to show community support following the events of 9/11. To Sandy, promoting assets in communities far and wide is indeed commonplace.

Sandy first heard about Developmental Assets in 1999, in relation to a neighborhood middle school. "This sounded like something I wanted to be part of," she says now. "It sounded very doable."

But Sandy thought that building assets should start at the primary school level. She became trained in assets and helped to start an Asset Committee at Pine Brook. She got parents involved and developed activities intended for students and their families. "Sandy is truly an individual who exudes all the qualities of an asset-building professional," says Susan Maginn, teaching assistant.

But it's not always easy. Some Pine Brook students are coping with parents who are separated or divorced. Many live in single-parent families. It isn't unusual for students to come to school on Mondays upset because of an incident over the weekend.

As Sandy herself says, "The kids bring a lot of baggage to school with them. We have to help them unpack that baggage before they're ready to start learning." Sandy and the other school adults do that by spending a lot of time talking and by being flexible with their schedules. If a student is upset, they let that student know that it's okay to be sad, and that working through those feelings is more important than completing a task. A counselor is also present in the building and will come into the classroom when necessary. Sandy believes strongly that building assets helps students unpack this baggage, and that it has to be continual.

Without question, Sandy does that. Says School Counselor Anne McAdam of Sandy: "Developing assets in children is in everything Sandy does. It is in all her interactions with them. She always looks for the positive and brings it out in a way that the children come to see the positives in themselves." Principal Patricia Dottore notes, "She always has time for every child. She listens to everything they have to say." And Assistant Principal Beth Boily is equally praising: "Sandy is warm, caring, and truly loves her students. They know that they are important in her eyes and that their contributions are valued."

Continual asset building is an important concept, and many of the teachers and administrators cited in this book say the same thing: Building Developmental Assets is not supplemental. It's integral. It's as much a part of teaching as homework, and it contributes as much to learning as homework. These educators view assets as essential components to students' academic achievement.

Within her own classroom, Sandy strives to expand the asset building in every direction. Every Monday, a senior citizen comes into the classroom to read with the students one-on-one. Every Friday, her students read with partners from a fourth-grade classroom. Many of her students have gone on to be fourth-grade "reading partners" themselves.

Each month, the class makes a paper classroom quilt based on stories that they've read, family traditions, or school activities. At the end of the school year, they design and make a real quilt to be donated to a local charity or facility. The students vote on where they'd like to donate the quilt.

Another end-of-the-school-year activity involves compiling a classroom cookbook that each family gets a copy of. Throughout the school year, families send in favorite recipes, and the students make each recipe, integrating language arts, science, and math.

During the year, students' parents also volunteer almost every day, and they also come to celebrations and parties (e.g., a pumpkin carving for science) and curriculum night. In addition, students' parents initial their children's reading logs and discuss with them what they've read.

All these activities are accompanied by information for students, parents, and teachers alike on how they relate to Developmental Assets— what assets are, which specific assets are being developed, and how people can build more assets.

Do they work? Do they help students academically? The successes of many of Sandy's former students, especially those who struggled, attest that they do. They return to Sandy's classroom to read to her current students. One boy, now in second grade, could barely write his name the year before. He contacted Sandy to "make an appointment" to read her class a story he'd written. He was so excited, says Sandy, that "he sat as proud as a peacock" when he read his story.

Another testament to success: Pine Brook Elementary School's significance as a great role model for building Developmental Assets. "Each of the 13 elementary schools in the district was asked to decide on a 'Signature' for their school," explains Pam. "For example, one of the schools is the 'Signature School for Math and Science.' . . . Pine Brook chose to be the 'Signature School for Developing Assets.'" Its mission now formally includes establishing and maintaining connections with students, teachers, families, and community members.

When you can truly commit to building assets for and with students, you're not only incorporating the asset framework into the curriculum, you're also building assets outside class, even outside school. Connecting to community is part of asset building, and Sandy's efforts have made a huge impact in that arena as well.

Sandy and her colleagues take care to keep Developmental Assets continually in front of their students and families, and into the larger community. The Asset Committee—which now comprises parents, teachers, administrators, and teaching assistants—meets monthly, and boy, do they get things done. They send home a list of the 40 Developmental Assets at the beginning of each school year, as well as monthly newsletters that focus on a specific asset and include an activity to support that asset. For example, in the "Constructive Use of Time" newsletter, children are asked to tell a story and draw a picture of themselves and a family member having fun. Parents are asked to describe three activities they enjoy doing with their children.

The committee also displays asset bulletin boards featuring all of the student, family, and staff activities that support the assets. It holds Assets Symposia—short conferences that focus on individual assets. And the school's expectations and rules have been aligned with the assets; for example: "Show respect of others through your words and actions," "Do your best so others can do their best," and "Accept responsibility for your actions."

And, as the following list shows, numerous of the asset-based activities that Sandy and her colleagues implement in the school spill over into the larger community:

> They participate in "Reflections," a national PTA program in which students choose to create literature, visual arts, music, or photography.
> They hold "Red Ribbon Week" to increase awareness of drug issues.
> They've collected more than $5,000 in the last four years through "Trick-or-Treat for UNICEF."
> They hold a summer reading program.
> They provide opportunities for students to become leaders, through Peer Mediation, Student Council, Safety Patrol, and Peace Builders.
> They facilitate a Pillow Project, in which each classroom designs and decorates a pillow; the pillows are then donated to local facilities, such as Ronald McDonald House, ARC of Monroe, and a variety of senior citizen homes.
> They put on "Open Up your Heart Month," in which they collect food and money for families in emergencies.
> They held a schoolwide "Diversity Day" to celebrate individual differences, including those of culture, ethnicity, and ability.

All these activities are explicitly labeled as asset builders. For example, the notice to parents about "Trick-or-Treat for UNICEF" notes, "Participating in Trick-or-Treat for UNICEF helps foster the assets of Caring Neighborhood, Caring School Climate, Service to Others, and Caring." And the flyers advertising "Open Up your Heart Month" cite the assets of Caring and Equality and Social Justice. As Teaching Assistant Susan Maginn says, Sandy is "extraordinarily well-connected with assets in the community."

But it's more than programs that makes the difference. Teacher Peggy Lawlor says about Sandy as a person:

> *I have worked with this elementary school teaching veteran for the past 11 years. She personifies the concept of asset building in every part of her personal and professional life. . . . She is one of the most caring and giving individuals I have ever known. . . . Sandy is warm, funny, and has a fantastic sense of humor. She has made positive connections with every colleague, student, and parent with whom she has worked.*

Lawlor goes on to describe how Sandy has sat on various building committees and worked closely with administration, staff, and parent stakeholders as everyone began to work on an asset initiative. She says that Sandy "lives the Developmental Assets every day."

Think about it: Students' lives don't end at 3:00 in the afternoon or on the borders of the school grounds. They live in their communities. And they'll continue to live in their communities at the end of the day, on the weekends, in the summer, and after they graduate. When teachers like Sandy promote assets in the community, they're making changes that are pervasive and long-lasting. Her efforts have made not only Pine Brook Elementary School rich with assets, but Greece, New York, as well.

> > >

asset-building teachers sustain a focus on Developmental Assets through relationships. The Developmental Assets framework is content as well as process, cargo as well as vehicle. It's one thing to incorporate assets into programs and help build them in individual students; it's quite another to sustain the emphasis on them when the programs and staff and students change. That's why establishing positive relationships is so key to nourishing and sustaining the building of assets. Because assets are not as much something to learn as someone to be, the task is less one of imparting knowledge than it is of setting an example.

mark hendrix

> GRADES 9, 10, AND 12
> GOLDEN SIERRA HIGH SCHOOL, GARDEN VALLEY, CA

Every day when he gets dressed in the morning, Mark Hendrix looks at a plaque that says, "You helped me figure out where all the pieces of the puzzle go." Given to him by a former student who had gone through a rough time, it's a thankful motivator that continues to help Mark be who he is—one of those teachers students seek out.

The student at the time several years ago was breaking up with her boyfriend, and her parents were getting divorced. Mark took her aside, listened to her, and prompted her with a few key questions: "Which parent are you closer with? Why don't you talk with her and tell her how you're feeling?" Three weeks later, the student had talked with her mother and was feeling better and performing better. Sometime after that, she gave Mark the plaque. The girl graduated and is now a graphic designer. She's one of many students who return to Mark after graduation to say thanks.

For Mark, establishing the relationship is primary. He believes that in order to educate a young person, you have to know what motivates that young person. And so he talks—and listens. Because he wants every student on campus to be able to talk to an adult at school, he goes into soph-omore classes and finds out which adults—including custodians, secre-taries, librarians, and every other school adult—students already seek out, and then he shares that information at staff meetings. In this way, school adults often become more aware that they're influencing students and can be more deliberate about offering them support in the future.

Jeanette Sargenti, currently the health education coordinator at the El Dorado County Public Health Department, had Mark as a teacher for all four of her high school years:

> *[He] always made sure that I knew that whether or not I chose to fail, succeed, be average, or stand out was entirely up to me; that teachers do not pass or fail you—it is always your choice. . . . He was also always at my side empowering me. Mr. H. does not stand in front of his students, he stands beside them. . . . The bottom line is that anytime I am now asked in my adult life how I have the skills I do, why I chose to work with young people, why I am so well rounded, balanced, etc., I always think of him. . . . I have never met someone who connects better with young people. He just plain "gets it."*

And get it Mark does. For 11 years, ever since he recognized that the incoming first-year student orientation was geared more toward parents than students, Mark has coordinated and now advises the Link Crew, which links senior leaders (after an application, interviews, and a two-day training) with students in grade 9. At the beginning of the year, instead of an orientation with lectures and rules, the Link Crew puts on a half-hour assembly, then hands off every 10 first-year students to two seniors.

The seniors have developed a list of 20 things they think students in grade 9 should know about Golden Sierra High School, and they share that list with them. They share advice both general (how to be a good person) and practical (how to take good notes, where to sit in class)—all information so that the new students can make the best out of their high school experiences. They progress through activities in the school for two hours, then they return for a 20-minute closing assembly together, with pizza and soda.

So right after the first day of school, first-year students have already formed the beginnings of relationships—with seniors, with some school adults, and with each other. Beyond the short-term benefit of making orientation more friendly, supportive, and relevant, this is a perfect way of passing on the asset framework from one "generation" of students to another.

Mark's asset-building efforts extend far beyond orientation. He's an extremely busy guy. Besides working with the Link Crew, he teaches English, social studies, and economics; he's coached football and baseball for 15 years; he's announced the school's football games for 21 years; he's adviser for the monthly school newspaper; and he's a member of the school's prevention advisory team, which coordinates programs and presentations regarding prevention and asset development. Thirteen years ago, he became the activities director. And six years ago, the school nurse asked him to take over the peer-helping program. The training focused on Developmental Assets, and he's been a believer ever since. It's obvious why he does all this: the students. "If you love the kids," he says, "they'll love you back."

Mark sets out to establish new (or further develop existing) relationships on the very first day of class. Each year, he gives a pop quiz:

1. Give me your entire full name.
2. Tell me why your parents named you that.
3. What do you want to be when you grow up?
4. How do you get to be that?
5. What kind of reader are you?
6. Tell me the last book that you read that you didn't have to.

For seniors:

7. Where are you going to be in one year?

That evening, Mark reads his students' responses, circles some of them, and makes comments, such as "This is cool" or "Go for it." Then he writes, "Welcome" (or "Welcome back" for returning students) at the bottom of the paper. He learns all his students' names, and he makes a poster of all the different jobs that students want to have.

Colleagues such as Darlene Wescombe and David Gray talk up Mark's genuineness, his enthusiasm and energy, and his ability to always be there for his students. He leads by example, and that can nourish and sustain the building of assets more than any lesson. As Mark says, "The majority of my teaching is being a role model. . . . You're always on stage."

Notes Jeanette Sargenti:

A great disservice that many adults and many teachers, in particular, do for young people is to talk at them, talk past them, provide a type of education that merely brings memorization and redundancy. . . . Often these people never realize the capability and creativity of young people. Mr. H. does the exact opposite. . . . He engages young people in every step of the process.

When asked if he uses any particular strategies for making connections with students for building Developmental Assets—while making sure that they meet academic standards—Mark replies, "Just listen." But it's more than that: "I personalize it," he says. "I use stories and experiences from my life to make it as real as possible—being a dad, a college graduate, a journalist."

He does that when he teaches economics, for example, by bringing in the newspaper and relating the curriculum to what's happening in students' lives: "What do you think about the California state budget?" "Which services should be dropped in order to reduce expenditures?" A student once suggested dropping school to save money, but then another student countered that you'd then need more money for jails and police. The discussion was on, and so was the learning.

In another example, Mark also has seniors make real budgets: "Where are you going to be in a year? How will you raise the money you need for rent?" He points out that credit card debt can ruin them— they wouldn't be able to buy a house. He shows how much interest they'd pay if they put $1,000 on credit.

The students appreciate it. Tiffany, a student last year, says, "He would speak to us in a normal conversation; it would apply to us more." Zack, a senior in Mark's journalism class, says, "He puts it in terms we'll understand." And Zack's mother, Susie, says, "He really empowers the kids. They basically do it. He's there for guidance."

But it's more than just guidance Mark provides. He knows how to relate to others and provide meaningful relationships. As Carmen, a former student, puts it:

> *I know one of the reasons he meant a lot to me [was] because he always took the time to care. He knew when all my athletic events were going to be and asked me about them afterward. He knew me well enough to know when I was having a bad day, and he always tried to make me feel better when I was. He made himself readily available for any student (including me on many occasions) who was having troubles in or out of school, and helped in any way he could. Mr. Hendrix was one of my biggest fans in everything I did in high school and was proud of me for, as well as in spite of, all the things I did. He truly cares about all his students and gives them the confidence and ability to go after all the things they dream about doing.*

You know that students are learning when they care, not because they're supposed to, but because they have a genuine attachment to someone or something. And that's what Mark epitomizes in his teaching.

For example, Mark comments, once the students working on the monthly school newspaper (called *The Bear Facts*—the school's mascot is the grizzly) see it get going, they begin to own it. They begin to care more about it. They get angry when they find someone's name has accidentally been misspelled!

Audrey Keebler, principal of Golden Sierra High School, confirms Mark's ability to sustain such relationships. Below are some of the things she says that Mark's students will say about him. (They'll probably remind you of other sections in this book.)

> "He understands what we are going through as teenagers, because he went through a lot of it himself. He is honest with us about life." *(Empathize with students.)*

> "He trusts us to assume leadership roles in the school; he guides us, but expects us to be independent. If we make mistakes, it's okay—we just learn and do better next time." *(Give students responsibilities.)*

> "He has high standards and expectations—an 'A' from Mr. Hendrix is a real accomplishment, not a gift." *(Challenge students.)*

> "He knows that engaged kids and busy kids are resilient kids and not in trouble on the street, so he keeps us engaged and busy. We are too tired to be on the street." *(Make the curriculum interesting.)*

> "He wants us to be successful adults and strong leaders, so he teaches the kinds of lessons (good grammar, good economics, good citizenship) that will help us be successful." *(Relate the curriculum to students.)*

What motivates Mark to continue listening, to continue trying to promote both academic achievement and asset building? "Two things," he says. "First, it feels like that's what I should do. And second, I really like my students. There are really good people underneath every one of them." Maybe expressions like those are why a lot of Mark's students tell him, "I don't ever want to disappoint you."

It's not that way with every student. One student editor had been radiating negativity and making life miserable for everyone around her. Mark tried to work with her. He told her, "It's not personal. I'm not reprimanding you because I don't like you." But she became angry, and she gave up. At the time, Mark says, he thought to himself, "Well, that's the way it goes." Three or four years later, he saw her brother in school and asked him how she was doing. "Tell her I said hi," said Mark. A month later, he got a letter of apology from the girl. "I was a total jerk," she wrote. It seems maybe Mark reached her after all.

caring teachers

> One of my little guys, Gary, said to me, "Mrs. Allen, even when
> I'm a big grown-up man and I'm even bigger than you, I will
> still always remember you in my heart." Tears welled up in
> my eyes as I gave him a big hug. I had a smile for the
> rest of the day. I still smile when I think about it.
>
> **PEGGY ALLEN**

*great teachers show they care by building relationships with their
students. Although this is the fourth quality of great teachers,
caring is in many ways the most important. It was how the teachers in this book were most often described by others, as well as
by themselves.*

*These teachers care about their students—not just as students, but as
people. These teachers listen to their students' ideas, they treat them with
respect, they attend their activities, they do them favors, they give them
responsibility, and they laugh, cry, play, work, get angry, celebrate, and
have fun with them—sometimes all in the same day.*

Peggy Allen is an extraordinary first-grade teacher in South Lebanon, Ohio. Pam Medzegian is an extraordinary high school teacher in Salem, Oregon. And Sue Walker is an extraordinary high school teacher in Gurnee, Illinois. For each of these three teachers, caring dominates all other factors.

Caring takes on different forms for different students, and that's probably as it should be. After all, if you adapt your teaching style to the student, then why not adapt your "caring style" to the student? It may be hugs for one, jokes for another, and intellectual challenge for a third. As you read the following profiles, think about the extent to which you care about your students and the ways you show that caring.

> > >

aring teachers nurture students. To many children, teachers are a major source of stability. Maybe these children are looking for something they don't receive at home, or maybe they're looking for that consistency that reminds them of what they do receive at home. What does it look like when a teacher is always there to help, to support, and to take care of her or his students? Caring teachers can be depended upon to offer the arm around the shoulder, the encouraging word, and the sage advice. They listen. They learn and grow along with their students.

peggy allen

> **GRADE 1**

> **SOUTH LEBANON ELEMENTARY SCHOOL, SOUTH LEBANON, OH**

Peggy Allen regularly invites four students at a time to join her after school for an afternoon of swimming and dinner, often pizza. It's not any particular occasion, big commitment, long event, or even an unusual idea—just a couple of hours between students and teachers. What *is* unusual is that these students are not her current students; they're *last year's* students.

One year out, she invites four at a time until she has made contact with every one of them. She still wants to know what they're doing, *how* they're doing, what she can help them with. These students truly know how much their former teacher cares about them—as do her current students.

Equally an uncommon occurrence—but typical behavior for Peggy—is her appearance at a current student's front door with a book, card, and throat lozenges. The student has been staying home from school with strep throat, a common occurrence for a first grader. Peggy truly cares about her students—outside the classroom, as well as in it.

You notice Peggy's caring for her current students in the classroom on two levels: On the curricular level, students take part in a myriad of activities in which they, not Peggy, are the focus. You get the definite impression that she cares about her students' varied learning styles, and thus tries to appeal to all of them while still making learning fun.

At the beginning of one particular spring day, some students are doing a "word search" at their desks, while others are looking at the six or seven butterflies that have recently emerged from their cocoons in a netted cage on the bookshelf. Then Peggy goes on to lead the class in some math problems concerning the butterflies.

The other level of caring—the personal level—is at least as impressive. Peggy takes an extra step in how she does things to make it caring. For example, sometime in the morning, a little girl is visibly upset because she's being teased about her middle name. Peggy consoles her, but rather than tower above her, she makes a point to kneel down to the girl's height and speak with her, arm around her shoulder. And what's more, Peggy reveals her own experiences with an unwanted middle name (*Sue*, as in *Peggy Sue*). The little girl nods in understanding, and the crisis is over.

And then there's the kind of caring that reaches the student as well as the child: How many times have you heard of teachers saying, "Okay, now, everyone choose a partner," to be followed by a mad scramble of boys and girls picking their favorite companions? Often, the result is that some students get paired with no one, while others know that they've been chosen only as a last resort. That's why Peggy always *assigns* partners. She knows what it's like to be on the outside, and she doesn't want children—especially vulnerable first graders relatively new to school—to feel that way. She at least can provide them safety and security, because, says Peggy, "They're so dependent on you for everything."

What's the root of all this caring? Peggy herself thinks it stems from something that happened to her in first grade. Her family had moved away for a year. As was the custom at the time, the school sent her records home, and it was up to her parents to take them to the next school. Peggy's teacher had written an extremely nice letter to her new teacher, saying that Peggy was special and bright. Peggy tears up as she relates this:

I never knew that about myself. . . . [After learning that,] I knew that I could be whatever I wanted to be. It just made so much difference to me. It showed me what an impact that could have. It always kind of stuck with me: If you were a teacher, you could build people up.

It was the "building people up" that motivated Peggy to become a teacher. Even now, when she thinks about her own experiences in elementary school, she doesn't remember work sheets or assignments or even activities; she remembers teachers and how they treated her. "The most important thing," she says, "is that these kids feel they're in a comfortable environment, safe and loved."

Are there teaching strategies for helping children feel safe and loved? How can you show someone how to be nurturing? When you watch teachers such as Peggy Allen, you begin to see how it's done—from the inside out. Peggy doesn't *do* nurturance; she *is* nurturance.

And caring, being nurturing, is part of being an asset builder and building assets. Erick Cook, principal of South Lebanon Elementary School, describes Peggy as "an asset builder of character," someone who empowers students to be a part of the decision-making process, who constantly praises them for the things they do, who encourages each child to participate in school activities, and who involves parents in their children's education. Cook believes that teachers need to listen well and to care about others, and Peggy exemplifies those characteristics.

An adherent of Developmental Assets, Cook wants to instill asset building as "second nature," and he's made sure that all his staff are familiar with the framework. Sometimes, he says, people think of the asset framework as just another program to implement. "But it's not that building assets is putting more programs on the plate," he maintains. "Assets *is* the plate." And serving up the plate is all about showing how you care.

Peggy first saw a poster of the 40 Developmental Assets at her local Y. She began wondering how many of the assets she actually built in her classroom. Reviewing the list, she could see that she focused on many of them; but she also realized that she could do much more. Since then, she's attended several awareness presentations on assets and has tried to become more intentional about building them.

On the evening before the first day of school, South Lebanon Elementary holds an open house every year. Several years ago, one little girl, Emily, hiding behind her parents, wouldn't say hello or look Peggy in the eye or speak at all. When at one point the girl and her mother walked to another part of the classroom, Peggy asked the father if the girl was always that shy. He said yes, she doesn't warm up to people and it would take her a long, long time to come out of her shell.

Peggy made it her mission to bring Emily out by earning her trust—and she did. It wasn't anything dramatic. Says Peggy, "I simply talk [with painfully shy children like Emily]—I accept nods and head shakes at first, and I'm doing most of the talking, but then I am able to ask questions that are more relevant and meaningful to them. . . . I always make it a point to comment on something they've done—a nice gesture in interacting with a classmate or the neatness of their work . . . just whatever I can do to build them up." By the end of October, the school was doing its annual play, *Big Pumpkin*. Emily was the witch—the lead role—and, in Peggy's estimation, she was "awesome."

In fourth grade now, Emily takes voice lessons and has appeared in several plays, including *The King and I* and *The Music Man* in Cincinnati. Peggy attended *The King and I* and opening the program to the pages introducing the actors, discovered that Emily thanked Peggy and said she got her start in *Big Pumpkin*. Typically, Peggy doesn't take credit for it: "I feel that I gave her a good start where she came out of her shell and felt safe and valued and no one would make fun of her, and she knew it was okay to speak up."

Peggy cares about students in all phases of their lives—picking them up in her own car in order to take them to presentations, sending home weekly newsletters, and involving parents in their children's progress and keeping them informed about when their children will be receiving awards. According to her colleagues, teachers Cindy Metzger and Sharon Hall, she seems to have an innate sense of her students' needs and potentials.

Vanessa's experience is indicative of that. Her son, Austin, was having difficulty reading. Peggy thought that Austin should be reading better and took him under her wing, where Austin flourished. At the end of the year, Austin both spoke and read at a PTA event. Vanessa says, "He was so proud of himself."

The voice of Debbie, the mother of the girl with strep throat, quavers when she talks about the scrapbook that she and every other parent of Peggy's students received in June—a scrapbook of photographs of their children taken throughout the school year, along with information such as their children's heights and career goals. It's something she'll keep forever.

Peggy's caring continues after school is out for the summer, too. She and her husband helped develop a monthlong, asset-based (Adult Role Models, Creative Activities, Youth Programs) summer program for 50 local, economically disadvantaged children in their community. Forty of the children had never been to an amusement park only two miles away. That quickly changed, as did the lives of all those children.

Spreading the word about building assets is something that Peggy's in an ideal position to do. As president-elect of her teachers union, she'll have ever-greater opportunities to spread the word among her colleagues. She's also spent most of her life in the South Lebanon area (about 30 miles northeast of Cincinnati). She knows the families, sees everyone constantly, and seems to be widely respected.

She uses her personal hobbies as an additional way to connect with kids, because she believes that her relationships with her students transcend the hours of the school day and the boundaries of the school campus. She's a runner—she recently competed in the annual "Flying Pig" marathon—and children will often see her preparing for a race and run with her. She also plays on three different softball teams during the year, and it's not unusual for students to attend some of those games, too.

When Peggy's students are asked what she does that makes them feel special and why they like her as a teacher, most of the responses reflect the idea of doing things together—Peggy sings with us, Peggy dances with us, and so on. One girl, however, sums it up best. It's Sidney, the girl who was teased about her middle name. "She gives us support," she says. "She's around if you need her."

When Peggy is asked what she likes most about teaching, she responds, "having the impact on kids' lives." Teachers have a tremendous impact on their students, even on the very youngest ones.

A girl who was once in Peggy's fourth-grade class recently graduated from college with a degree in finance and e-mailed Peggy. She wrote to tell her how much she remembered the fourth grade and how much she appreciated what Peggy did for her. They're corresponding regularly now.

A more recent student wrote to her, "You have done a good job teaching me to be a better reader in reading class. You are very kind and care a lot about all of your students." Note that he said she cared about *not just him but all of her students.*

That kind of feedback helps Peggy immeasurably: "I am always questioning myself, doubting myself, and I really need those words of encouragement for reassurance. Maybe that's why I can relate to these kids so well. I think they need the same thing."

> > >

Caring teachers value students. We treat things we value differently than other things. We take care of them. We're proud of them. It's the same with people we value. It's not one particular act or gesture; it's the routine respect that you accord your students. Students know when you value them by your day-to-day interactions. Do you honestly consider their opinions? Do you follow through with what you tell them? Do you seek their advice? Young people have much to offer; caring teachers recognize this and let their students know they recognize it.

pam medzegian

"Home isn't an address but a state of mind" is how one of Pam Medzegian's students in her Peer Mentoring Program sums up the environment Pam creates. The entire feeling is one of comfort, like a family whose members know each other very well.

It's 6:30 on a Tuesday morning in April, and students from Pam's Peer Mentoring Program are excited. They're planning a surprise birthday party for one of their peers, and they go about it with the same giddy earnestness that characterizes much of the rest of their activities.

They're gathering in a hive of offices in the basement of one part of South Salem High School, which comprises 1,750 students in grades 9 through 12. There is one large room divided into four areas—one with chairs set up for meetings, another with couches, a third with a couple of computers, and a fourth that actually looks like an office. Students are self-directed: One of them writes up a report on a computer, another reads from a textbook, while still others prepare to greet the birthday honoree.

Pam herself could be one of the students. Everyone who comes in greets her with a hug, a quip, or some sort of repartee. She barks out commands but follows them with a wink, a smile, or a "love you."

All the students are more than happy to talk about Pam. Natasha says that Pam is like "a second—or first—mom," and that she's "one of the most selfless people I know." Leana says that Pam promotes a trusting, one-on-one environment, and that "this is her passion, her life." And Susan says that she knew Pam cared about her because Pam always asked about how she was doing:

> *"Why are you dressed up today?" "Why are you tardy?" She is always giving out sincere compliments and tells us that she loves us. Then she follows up her words with actions. She asks about our*

lives and listens to our responses. She spends countless hours not getting paid just to spend time with us. She calls us when we're sick, remembers our birthdays, and invites us over to her house. And she also doesn't let us get away with stuff. She demands our best and won't take less. She cares enough to help us succeed.

This is another side of caring: the things you do and say that let students know they really matter. As with nurturance, it has to be genuine in order to work. Students know when they are genuinely valued and when the value is faked.

Pam can certainly recognize false caring. The seed of her desire to value children was probably planted when she realized at age 5 that her kindergarten teacher acted as if children were invisible.

The seed sprouted a year later when she managed to jump rope 99 times. Along with the feeling of accomplishment came the idea that she might want to be a physical education teacher. Later, in middle and high school, some positive role models reinforced her initial inclinations to teach.

The road to the Peer Mentoring Program took several interesting turns. At first, it was thought that P.E. teachers could make social connections with students more easily than other teachers could, so Pam and others at South Salem High School started "Freshman House." "Freshman House" is where one team of teachers meets once a day on behalf of one-half of the first-year students who have their core classes in the morning ("AM House") and another team of teachers meets once a day on behalf of the remainder of grade 9 students who take their core classes in the afternoon ("PM House"). The teachers are able to know their group more personally.

"Freshman House" evolved into a Community of Learners—older students teaching younger students. Then they started Freshman Fun Day— 500 students playing games led by other students. The natural extension of that activity was peer mentoring, in which sophomores, juniors, and seniors help out first-year students. It is establishing just such a program, a peer mentoring program, that is a key example of adults valuing young people and helping prepare them to own their education.

The Developmental Assets framework fit perfectly into what Pam was doing. She first heard about assets six years ago from a Marion County family commissioner, who thought that her program was reflective of assets. Once she learned about assets herself, Pam realized that "incorporating assets is a natural connection. The assets fall into place when you make the connections. The service-learning wraps it up."

Now, all her students know about assets through the Peer Mentoring Program and in her "Personal Relationships" class; moreover, they pass it on to others. Leana, one of the peer helpers, says that Pam and students have attended Search Institute's Healthy Communities • Healthy Youth (HC • HY) conference three years in a row. Last year in California, four of the peer mentors and Pam presented a diversity training that reaped the highest attendance of any station at an HC • HY conference.

As Pam herself says, "If they're valued, kids can be so empowered." That's the core of the Developmental Assets framework: helping students find and build on their own strengths so that they can do the same for others. When a teacher like Pam shows her students that she values them, soon they start to believe that they're valuable.

That empowerment is very obvious when you talk with Pam's students. They're assured, they're friendly, they're courteous, they're conscious of what they've accomplished, and they're aware of the potential they have to affect others. One of the mentors, Kari, says that having kids open up to you for the first time is "incomparable" and she hadn't realized the role she was in before that. Says another student, Leana:

Zig [Pam] goes above and beyond the role of a teacher, becoming a natural inspiration, role model, friend, and mentor. She loves what she does and puts all her effort into empowering and inspiring the lives of youth. She dreams that students will see their potential and embrace the opportunities that come to them in life, making them strong and capable people. I know she has affected my life and inspired me to do my best in everything. I know that I can do anything if I really want to, and of course I always know I can seek her out for a little support or guidance. Pam Medzegian is a great

example of a teacher who implements the 40 assets into her teach-
ing. It's just part of who she is, making a difference in the lives of
youth every day.

Pam now has 130 mentors, 22 leaders, and four administrators. More
than 200 students a year usually apply to be mentors. If selected, they
have to keep up their grades to remain mentors. Pam chooses 40 for the
class, "based on their passion and their ability to be role models."

They have summer retreats for the administrators, who in turn train
the leaders, who in turn facilitate the peer mentoring class. Four days a
week, the leaders mentor and tutor in South Salem's ninth-grade classes
and in other schools.

The administrators export the program, along with the assets.
They've started programs in places as diverse as Montana and Ukraine.
(Pam believes that the more you get out in the community with youth
developers, the more you know about different resources; she heard
about an exchange program with Ukraine run by Western University,
in nearby Monmouth, Oregon, and acted on it).

The mentors also instruct middle school trainings in peer mediation
and peer counseling. They work at Boys and Girls Club facilities, address-
ing conflict management in fifth grade and bullying and harassment in
lower grades.

For seven years, Pam taught P.E. as well as peer mentoring. She used
to teach P.E. most of the day, while the peer mentors would run the class
and communicate with her by walkie-talkie. But after several years, she
gave up P.E. and coaching to devote herself full time to peer helping and
Developmental Assets. As Pam says, "Kids need to have someone consis-
tently working with them; they deserve that."

Recently, one peer mentor, Sheena, went with some other peer mentors to the Oregon Youth Summit, a leadership conference at Seaside,
Oregon. The mentors soon discovered that many of the students there
were "pretty rough"—in appearance as well as behavior—but they deter-
mined to get rid of all their "negative stuff" concerning those who were
different from them.

In particular, they met a girl who conveyed ruggedness from every facet of her being. Sheena says that they tried to look past the girl's exterior and get to know her. Later, in the girls' room, the mentors talked about how nice the girl was. The girl overheard them and broke down crying. Eventually, she shared a journal with them, and the mentors had made a friend. Sheena herself was originally very shy, but now, she says, she's the opposite.

Eric Johnson, a former Spanish teacher at South Salem High School, says that Pam's peer helpers inspire other students by acting as role models. He said that one peer mentor, after talking to Eric's class, left his name and e-mail address for others to contact him. He notes that students who are at first shy, but then receive applause for saying something, become more talkative. Now Eric himself has started to teach peer helping.

Cherri is a parent of one of the mentors. She says that the program "pulled stuff out" of her son that he had already. He now has a lot of confidence, particularly because of public speaking. Cherri says that Pam "acts like a kid, relates to them," and "raises the bar" for them. Once, when Pam was sick, Cherri had 20 of Pam's students over at her house. "I was amazed," she says, at how independently and quietly they worked.

It's also not always easy running a nontraditional program. Pam starts one of her classes at 6 in the morning; it's the only time of the day that the students in the International Baccalaureate Program can participate. Parents—and teachers—don't always understand why students have to work on projects and attend retreats, in addition to (and sometimes instead of) attending classes.

Pam tries to counter these feelings by encouraging parents to join in the activities and showing teachers and administrators where her curriculum has met college standards (e.g., for community service and health). She now has documentation that her peer mentoring class can meet the standards of seven different college courses.

Emphasizing students' academic achievement along with everything else is extremely important to Pam. She recently received an e-mail from a former student, now in college. Pam tells the story:

This is a young lady that was raised by her grandmother till five years of age, when her grandma died. Her mom had a drug problem, and she doesn't know much about her dad. She was then taken in by her aunt and [her aunt's] boyfriend, and then ended up living with a friend her senior year. She overcame so many obstacles, earned a high GPA, was awarded "Volunteer Student of the Year" for the State of Oregon last year, and was given scholarship money and a trip to Washington, D.C. She was also selected as "Optimist of the Year" in the Salem/Keizer District. She is sought out to make presentations in national conferences and throughout the city regarding mentoring.

When she was a sophomore, we met as she became a mentor, then a leader, and then was selected to be one of our four administrators last year. She was quiet and shy at first and not filled with much confidence. . . . We became friends and she called me "Mom." I attended her functions, went shopping with her, made sure she had jewelry for her prom, wrote about her as a mom would in last year's yearbook, and just had the honor of accompanying her to college on her first day.

Here, in part, is what the girl had to say in her e-mail:

I really wanted to tell you something. Okay, so I'm taking a leadership class and a communication class here at U of P. It's so funny because it's everything we ever covered in class, all of the lessons and trainings that I taught, put together, and naturally picked up during peer mentoring. All of the students in my classes are desperately struggling, while I'm just kickin' back and lovin' being the teacher favorite. . . . In communication, I just wrote a five-page paper on "What are the elements that make up communication?" in only two hours. I haven't gotten my grade back, but I'm pretty sure it'll be great. People in that class were telling me how they stayed up until three in the morning just trying to write three pages.

I guess what I'm getting at is, "Thank you." Thank you for teaching me so much and giving me the opportunity to advance. . . .

*I have learned vital lessons that will forever be useful. It wasn't
something I really realized until I was gone, so "Thank you, Pam!"
I have decided to minor in communication. . . .*

*Also, the people skills, listening and leadership skills have
made it so much easier to start over here and make all new friends.
I absolutely love it.*

Pam's pride was tremendous. In comparison, when another student
wasn't making choices consistent with the goals of the mentoring program, Pam took it as a personal failure. She consequently had to drop
him from the program, and the student's family got upset about it. Pam
realizes that "I can't put my expectations on them. I want to love them
for who they are and not what I expect them to become." Nonetheless,
it's hard to brush off, and Pam admits that sometimes it's difficult to
maintain her positive attitude when those kinds of things happen.

Pam will tell you that her goal is for her students to "take ownership
of their education." And clearly, when students feel cared for and valued,
they can do so much more readily. Says Susan, a current student:

*[Pam] is a light in the darkest places and she is ridiculously good
at what she does. She understands that kids are immature, silly,
unfocused, and overcommitted. She understands this but also
understands that they deserve respect and will only rise to the level
that you permit and encourage them to reach. She loves with a
divine love that spills out of her and gets everyone close soaking wet.*

Samantha Ragaisis, former assistant principal of South Salem
High, puts it even more directly when she says of Pam, "She's brought
the whole child into our school. Whatever is best for kids, she'll do."
Adds current Vice-Principal Cheryl Hagsteth:

*The peer mentors are a group of young adults who not only strive
to become leaders, but through Pam's guidance, achieve. I have
relied on the peer mentors throughout the year to assist with the
coordination of important curricular events. Never once have
I been disappointed as they work relentlessly to provide excellence*

in their service, maturity, and confidence in their communication and compassion in their interactions. Under Pam's direction, students are given opportunities and experiences which help define who they are and what they will become. The students will become inspirational leaders, and highly contributing adults and members of society.

> > >

Caring teachers believe in students. Believing in students means that you care enough about them to help them become the best persons they can be. Believing in students means you choose to believe each one has the potential for becoming a happy, healthy, productive adult. It means that you look for the strengths in all your students, you encourage them to overcome the negative influences in their lives, you don't give up when they get in trouble, and—especially—you don't give up when the *student* has given up.

sue walker

> GRADES 11 AND 12
> WARREN TOWNSHIP HIGH SCHOOL, GURNEE, IL

At his high school graduation, Tony lamented to his peers that he could never say no to his teacher, Mrs. Walker; but in the same breath, this once-shy boy added to her, "I don't ever want to have to say no to you."

Why? Because he knew that Sue believed in him, that she cared enough about him to look beyond his shyness, to focus on something even he might not have been aware of: his potential. Sue Walker nurtured and pushed him because she cared about him. She kept asking him to do things, kept giving him increasing amounts of responsibility because she valued who he was.

And by the time Tony graduated, he'd been editor of the school newspaper, president of the local business organization, and recipient of the school's "Most School Spirit" award. At his graduation party, Tony's grandfather came up to Sue and said, "I can't believe what you've done with this boy!"

Believing in a student is perhaps the ultimate in caring, because you're caring for the student not only in the here and now but also in the what-could-be future. That's how Sue Walker relates to her students. She sees each of them as a project unfolding, a flower yet to bloom, a scholar in the making.

Nancy Marion, the coordinator of the Developmental Assets initiative in Gurnee, Illinois, says that Sue

> *immediately comes to mind as the best example in my life of an asset-building teacher. I have developed a wonderful partnership with Sue and have seen her interact with her students firsthand. They flock to her to tell her about their problems and she listens with her heart. Her classroom is a hangout after school for students to work on projects, discuss the next social event, or dream up a new adventure. It is not uncommon to find her in the classroom with her students long after the last bell has rung.*

Hanging out in a classroom with students is not originally what Sue thought she wanted to do. She wanted to become an accountant, but her mother encouraged her to be a teacher instead. (Sue waited a generation; her daughter is an accountant.) She got a teaching scholarship and began teaching after college. She now teaches an accounting/word-processing elective for students in grades 11 and 12. About half her class is in Future Business Leaders of America (FBLA), of which she's the prime sponsor. The chapter is the largest in the country, with about 700 students.

Five years ago, Warren Township High School—about 3,500 students—conducted Search Institute's *Profiles of Student Life: Attitudes and Behaviors* survey, and the district became partners with a Healthy Communities • Healthy Youth initiative.

When the results of the survey were shared with the students in Warren Township High School and they saw which assets were high and low, they said that the asset they wanted to work on most was Community Values Youth. Consequently, Sue's FBLA group does a lot of community service—for example, tutoring seniors and visiting a halfway house for people who have HIV.

Sue also keeps a bulletin board in her class of newspaper articles featuring students. She encourages coaching and small-group work in her classes. She wants to teach students initiative and responsibility. She asks students for feedback and evaluation. She tries to make it to sporting events, even though she doesn't particularly enjoy them—especially wrestling. Yet, she knows that the relationships she has with her students are helped by the extracurricular activities she attends. As Sue says, "It's a whole way of showing respect. They care so much that I'm there."

Dana, once also very shy, can vouch for Sue's caring. Though she was born in Colorado, Dana has spent most of her life in Abu Dhabi and came to Sue's class as a grade 9 student.

Before I knew Mrs. Walker, I used to admire her sense of humor at Future Business Leaders of America meetings. I was a freshman trying to get involved and meet people, and she was so welcoming and inviting at these meetings. She would always have a smile on her face or be joking about something.

As I started working more closely with Mrs. Walker, not only did she have a tremendous effect on me, but I could see the effect she has on every student she teaches, every teacher she talks to, or every passerby in the hallway.

I remember once when my car would not start after a long day and evening at school; she cheered me up like no other. I was so frustrated about this ugly Geo Metro—that I still do own—and I came back into her room in tears over this petty incident. She was so understanding and comforting. She kept cracking jokes to make me laugh, and I know that on that day she was swamped with

schoolwork and grading, but she put it all down until she was
certain that I felt better.
    This woman builds people.

Dana received an award for her community service and returned
from college to talk to Sue's students about her high school experiences
and what a difference they made. From Sue's standpoint, it was remark-
able watching this shy girl turn into "an amazing young lady."

Brenda Dunn Kinney is president of her own business and became
a mentor for some of Sue's students. Over the years, she's come to know
Sue and respect her enormously. "I've not met one person," she says,
"like Sue Walker—ever. She gives of herself selflessly. When kids need
her, she's always there for them." It is such caring, such believing in others' potential, that helps these students succeed.

A project in particular that Brenda refers to is one that she and Sue
were working on with three girls. The assignment was to write a business plan and present it, and they were working with the girls on trying
to find their voice. One of the girls succeeded even beyond their expectations: She won a Fulbright scholarship to Howard University and
eventually became "Future Business Leader of the Year" for the state
of Illinois.

Sue believed in these students. She believes in students that others
may have given up on. She believes in students who may have given up
on themselves.

Swapnil, who came to Sue's class last year, is from India. His accent
was so strong that sometimes Sue would have to ask him to write down
what he was saying. Like Dana, he was very shy.

Sue encouraged him to compete in an accounting contest at the
nearby College of Lake County. After explaining to his parents what Sue
wanted him to do and getting their permission, he entered the contest
and placed fifth out of the whole county. He was really nervous and so
unaccustomed to a "moment in the sun" that he wasn't even sure how to
shake hands with the people who congratulated him.

He sent the following e-mail to Sue. When you read the e-mail, think about what it means to a young student—new to a school, new to class-mates, new to a culture—to have someone like Sue care about him and believe in him:

> *Hello Mrs. Walker,*
>
> *I'm very very sorry . . . I don't know what happens to me when I go in front of people.*
>
> *Today on the stage . . . I did not shake hand properly . . . I'm sorry . . . for that . . . . I get very nervous when I go in front of people . . . I could not speak . . . anything . . . my legs start trembling . . . I don't know . . . I get feared . . . so I behaved . . . such . . .*
>
> *I had to work for the competition . . . but I think . . . the other thing which really helped me a lot today . . . was YOU. . . .*
>
> *THE WAY U ALWAYS . . . SAID ME U WILL BE FINE . . . AND . . . DON'T WORRY . . . I'M VERY VERY VERY THANK-FUL TO YOU . . . FOR YOUR SUPPORT AND CONFIDENCE IN ME. . . .*
>
> *I READ UR MAIL YESTERDAY . . . AFTER I CAME FROM THE REVIEW SESSION . . . AND I FELT BETTER . . . TODAY AGAIN IN THE MORNING . . . U SAID ME U WILL BE FINE . . . DON'T WORRY. . . .*
>
> *THANK YOU VERY MUCH ONCE AGAIN . . . YOU PLAYED A BIG ROLE IN THIS THING . . . FOR ME.*

Such letters, says Sue, "are the things that make me keep doing it," keep teaching. And while she notes that "the assets didn't surprise me," she's quick to emphasize that she sets up rules and expectations for her students because "I have high expectations of my students and their behavior." As Sue adds, "The minute you lower your expectations for children, they lower theirs. As a teacher, you're a role model." Having high expectations clearly is the explicit manifestation of caring and believing; you're saying to students, "Here's what I think you can do."

hardworking
teachers

> *I can't imagine being just a teacher.*

KARRIE DOCTERMAN

*a*ll teachers work hard; that's the nature of the job. All the teachers in this section are hardworking, just as all the teachers in this book are trusting, engaging, asset-building, and caring. Martha Roper, Karrie Docterman, and Kim Rampmeyer appear in this section because they represent an interesting cross section of teachers who work hard.

Martha, who teaches in the same school as Andie Brown, not only teaches sex education classes but also contributes professionally in many ways to the greater St. Louis community. Karrie, in Spokane, Washington, seems to be at the forefront of all things assets. And Kim, in Anchorage, Alaska, teaches an inordinate number of classes and participates in dozens of events throughout the year.

Each of these teachers, in her own style, works far above and beyond what most people would consider standard. For these teachers, working hard at their jobs means working especially hard at building connections.

It's these connections—with their students, within their schools, within their communities—that make a difference in the lives of their students and in their own lives as well.

None of these teachers feels externally *compelled to put in the extra hours, attend the events, have the one-on-one discussions, or visit students' families. They do it because they want to do it. They do it because they get something out of it. They do it because it helps them make authentic connections with their students, have a positive impact on them, and truly make a difference. As you know from your own experience, work that's enjoyable isn't a burden.*

Consider what you currently do and what you would enjoy doing *to help build assets for and with your students. What's in it for you? How can you receive the satisfaction that all these teachers receive when they realize they've made a positive impact on a young person?*

> > >

hardworking teachers build connections with students. They recognize that each student is an individual, with distinct abilities, attitudes, and experiences, and as such needs to be treated accordingly. This is where the hard work comes in. Building connections with students requires you to form and maintain genuine, supportive, respectful relationships—even with those students whom you may not like, even with those students who may not like you. It doesn't mean that you can't have a bad day or that you have to give in to every student's wishes. But keeping the connections open and meaningful requires vigilance and focus.

martha roper

> **GRADE 10**

> **PARKWAY SOUTH HIGH SCHOOL, MANCHESTER, MO**

For Martha Roper, working hard is about intensely focusing on what's most important and effective:

Teaching inside this classroom is a full-time job. I notice that [some] principals value teachers more who sponsor canned food drives or who coach cheerleading (all good asset builders), but I am not going to let anyone move me off my target population: my own class list.

When I used to sponsor big events, it took me away from those asset-building moments one-on-one with kids that change their lives, and I just decided to stop trying to be teacher of the year. I stopped giving all the workshops and teaching the graduate classes in favor of being a teacher who has time to sit and listen and help kids after school.

Part of her success in asset building, says Martha, "is the boundaries I set in my job and going with my strengths." She uses the analogy of tennis: She knows that her forehand is a strength, so she has learned to put even more topspin on it so that she can make the best of that strength. She does the same with her students: helping them recognize and making the best of their strengths.

In part, Martha does this by being protective of her students at Parkway South High School, located in a middle-class suburb of St. Louis: "They need to know the scary things out there," she says, "and they need to know how to use their assets to reach out and move forward to be healthy."

Martha is a strong believer in the Developmental Assets framework, particularly as it relates to prevention. "I just can't be yelling at kids not to do drugs and sex," she says. "I have to be giving them something positive, something better." What that something positive, something better is, is building assets on a small scale. So, in part, Martha asks them to look up Search Institute on the Internet and develop a lesson plan in small groups, assigning an asset category to each group. They find articles on the assets, write a skit about typical experiences and situations, and find ways to get support in their lives.

Most teachers who help students build assets will tell you that it comes down to this: a relationship between two people. This can't be overestimated. You can provide the supportive environment, you can implement the programs that give students opportunities to succeed, but you can have the most impact when you interact, one-to-one, with a young person. That can be difficult when you have a million other things to do—but that's what Martha works hard to do, nonetheless.

Her schedule includes teaching five classes for 18 weeks, and one homeroom—an academic lab for students with a range of GPAs—for four years. In addition, she'll help the occasional club and do committee work for professional development, faculty meetings, and so on, but to give her all to students in her classes, she doesn't coach or go on trips, and tries to say no to similar major commitments. Instead, she focuses on making extensive notes about each student and that student's parents, and she checks her list and hands out "gifts" of time and expertise.

For example, she writes to returning students several times during the summer. She mails invitations to parties at her homeroom—say, on the first day of school—and she orders pizza: "It makes them feel special," she says.

In the fall, she makes sure that she communicates with each student's parent. She lets them know she'd like to be their children's surrogate mother at school. At the open house, she asks parents to brag about their children.

Brandon, a 10th grader, explains how he got "double-pressured" by his mother and Martha: The two of them worked together to come up with a study plan for him, in which his mother signs his completed assignments. Brandon actually appreciates this effort and says that Martha is like a second mother. He thinks that having a relationship with a school adult is often considered not very cool, but he says that you have to shrug off peers who ridicule you for that.

So that she always knows about her students—their strengths, their backgrounds, their personalities—Martha works to keep a "rolling calendar of connections." She tells them her story, how no one ever talked to her about her life, about what mattered, about how to get a good grade. And making it clear how available she is to her students, she says, "Don't you ever say that no one sat you down and said, 'I care about you. I care about your achievements. I am here for you.' Here's my e-mail address. Here's my cell phone number."

Mya, a freshman, likes the way Martha works hard to stay connected with them—by giving students her cell phone number, by giving them presents on their birthdays, and by calling home when they're absent to make sure that they're okay.

That said, very few parents or students contact her during her personal time. A couple of years ago, a senior boy knocked on her door at 10:00 on a Saturday night. He said that he'd just had unprotected sex; what could he do? Such instances are rare; for the most part, Martha's interactions with students occur at school, on the phone, or in letters.

And those interactions are powerful. A year ago, one of Martha's students had moved from a family in which her mother was a prostitute and drug addict. The girl's father and his new wife adopted her. At any mention of a sexual nature in health class, the girl would actually hiss, and her body would recoil. She complained to her father, to the principal, to the counselor. She gave Martha a letter she had written complaining about her teaching style. She wanted to drop out of her class.

Martha asked if instead she could get to know her, under the premise that "If you know I care, then maybe you'll care about what I know." Martha soon realized that the girl was motivated to get good grades, and so she taught her how to use PowerPoint computer software. Soon, the girl's confidence increased. For her part, Martha relented a bit on the sex talk and gave the girl permission to leave the room if she got uncomfortable.

The girl created and gave a PowerPoint presentation on poverty and health. She explained what it was like to grow up poor, without money to buy a CD, sometimes without even electricity. In 18 weeks, she was completely turned around: She was proud of her competence in PowerPoint, and her discomfort with the class discussions about sex lessened. She received an A in the class.

With a perverse pride, Martha tells you that she came to teaching via the "dumb blonde" track. Her older brother and sister were reared to be intellects, but by the time Martha came along, her mother's advice had become less focused on academics. Instead, she told the young Martha that it was good for her to be social, but that she didn't have to get great grades. So why did Martha go into education? Besides the fact that her mother, grandmother, and great-grandmother all taught, she was given this sage advice (not too uncommon in previous generations): "If your husband leaves you, you can make a career teaching—it's a good job for a woman."

Martha received a B.S. in education from Texas Christian University and moved to New York with her husband—who was attending Union Theological Seminary—when she was six months pregnant. A couple of months later, she was taking a class on death and dying and befriended an 80-year-old man. He offered to pay her tuition for her first graduate school course, if she would do the same for someone else. Three years later, she got her master's in family and community relations from Columbia University Teachers College, and she's never forgotten the support she received when she most needed it.

A partial list of Martha's achievements would seem to render that early maternal warning immaterial—as much as her concerns about trying to do it all:

> During the mid- to late 1970s, the health class she taught at University City High School was identified as one of the top 10 sexuality education programs in the country.
> Since 1978, she has been a frequent guest on KMOX Radio in St. Louis, discussing sexuality and answering listeners' questions.
> From 1982 to 1994, she trained teachers in the Webster University Master of Arts in Teaching Program.
> In 1985, *St. Louis* magazine listed her as one of the 50 outstanding St. Louisans under the age of 40 who were making a difference.
> In 1990, she was one of only two American schoolteachers who were selected to serve on the U.S. delegation to the World Health Organization conference on AIDS.
> In 1992, the Association for the Advancement of Health Education named her the "National Health Education Professional of the Year."
> In the early 1990s, she served on the National Sexuality Education Guidelines Task Force convened by the Sex Information and Education Council of the United States.
> In 1994, 1998, and 2004, she was listed in *Who's Who among America's Teachers*.
> In 2000, she was invited to advise the U.S. Surgeon General on policy directions the U.S. Centers for Disease Control and Prevention should take to promote sexual health.
> In 2001, she and her husband, Dr. Peter C. Scales, jointly received the "Lifetime Professional Service" award from Planned Parenthood of the Greater St. Louis Area.
> Her work has been reported on in *Parents* magazine, *Family Circle,* and *U.S. News & World Report,* and she has appeared on *CBS Sunday Morning.*

Even her sports accomplishments speak to her working hard: In 2002, she won the gold medal in the pole vault at the St. Louis Senior Olympics and at the Missouri Senior State Games—in both cases the first woman ever to do so—topping that off with the *national* gold medal the next year.

Martha is clearly immersed in her role as educator and is incredibly successful at it. But what's really hardworking about Martha is that she builds many, many individual connections with students. Sometimes that's easier with older high school students than with younger elementary school students; the students are more developed, more complex, so they can be more receptive. On the other hand, sometimes it's more difficult; because the students are more developed, more complex, they can be more elusive.

One morning, for example, Martha's health class starts with a student having to make a decision: She's scheduled to present a report to the class, but she's not prepared. Martha gives her a choice: Deduct 50 points out of a possible 500 for not having specific citations, or deduct 100 points for not having the report done at all. The girl gives the report.

Next, someone reads aloud from the book *Succeed Every Day* by Pamela Espeland (Free Spirit Publishing, 2000), while students are asked to relax, perhaps close their eyes, and try to relieve any stress. They're then invited to share any recent experiences. One student says that she's been tense because a day earlier she drove over a curb and into a neighbor's mailbox; she now has to pay for repairs to the car and put in a new mailbox.

Martha then distributes the "Science Times" section from the *New York Times*. After several minutes, students discuss the articles they've read, receiving "participation points" for having done so. The thing that's extraordinary about the class is that academics and engagement blend perfectly. Students are learning, and they seem to be enjoying it.

Martha's two other health classes this day include small groups coming up with solutions to drinking/driving accidents, a girl giving a quite explicit PowerPoint presentation on sexually transmitted diseases, another student giving a report on the "morning-after pill," and students using cell phones to role-play breaking up with each other. Throughout it all, Martha peppers students with questions, makes provocative comments, shares her opinions, and stirs them to think.

Such thinking doesn't go unnoticed by parents, either. One parent, Bob, whose son Thomas is one of Martha's students, says that his politics are diametrically opposed to Martha's, but that he respects her, because she tolerates differing viewpoints from students "without penalty." "She's motivated by concern for her students," he says, noting how she works hard to go "over and above the normal teacher in caring for kids." At one point, Martha knew that Thomas didn't swim very well at a state swim meet and called home to express concern about him. Bob says he appreciated that immensely.

On the other hand, there are stories that are less than successes: One ninth-grade homeroom student, who weighed 75 pounds, was learning disabled and in need of a lot of help as early as possible. Unfortunately, he didn't get it from his mother, who apparently forgot to send him to school for the first two days of the year. The following year, Martha wrote several cards home to remind him to show up for the beginning of the year. It didn't happen; the family had gone surfing in Hawaii.

In the boy's junior year, Martha again sent cards to his home. He didn't show up for the first two weeks; this time, they went surfing in California. Because of disagreements over the content of Martha's health class, the boy's mother eventually moved him to another class, although he's still in Martha's homeroom. This year, his last in high school, he finally did come to school on the first day. Martha continually tries to have a positive relationship with him. All she wants to communicate—to parents as well as to students—is "I am there for them."

Despite such roadblocks, Martha continues to do just that—to be there for them. Mya, the first-year student, sums up the feeling that's shared by many of Martha's students: She feels sure that Martha "won't let anything bad happen to me." All the hard work aside, it's easy for Martha to be there for them, because she loves her work—for her, the students are the work, as well as her wards, her responsibilities.

As for her responsibility to help pay for someone else's graduate school expenses—remember the man who offered to pay Martha's tuition for her first graduate school class if she would do the same for someone else? Well, with a little money and lots of "encouragement" gifts and emotional support, she did! Dr. Bevanne Bean-Mayberry, who was one of Martha's students, is currently an internist at the Veterans Administration Hospital of the University of Pittsburgh Medical School, where she's also on the faculty. She's married to a pediatric cardiologist and has three little boys. Martha is her mother figure, her mentor—she's also her friend.

> > >

hardworking teachers build connections throughout the school. Just as engaging teachers involve first the students, then the school, and finally the community; just as asset-building teachers incorporate Developmental Assets into first the school curriculum, then the school environment, and finally the community environment; so it is with hardworking teachers, who build connections first with students, then throughout the school, and finally throughout the community. When you build connections throughout your school, you're giving yourself a break. If for some reason you can't be there for a student—and no one can be there for everyone all the time—then maybe someone else can. That person might be another teacher, the principal, a counselor, a secretary, a coach, a nurse, a bus driver, a librarian, or even another student. When you build connections throughout the school, no student will be without someone who's a supporter and an asset builder.

karrie docterman

> **GRADES 9, 10, 11, AND 12**
> **ROGERS HIGH SCHOOL, SPOKANE, WA**

Karrie Docterman had wanted to be a veterinarian, but decided to change career plans when she passed out during a job shadowing. The animals' losses are our children's gains, because for the past nine years, Karrie has taught students of the human persuasion; and they've benefited tremendously as a result.

Karrie teaches at Rogers High School, in the northeast, rather rough, section of Spokane, Washington. She's also an alumna of Rogers, and, as Youth Empowerment Project (YEP) Coordinator Piper Anderson puts it, "chose to go back to her old stomping grounds to make a difference."

Two years ago, the City/County Youth Department approached the school with a large project in mind. Together with YEP, Karrie dove into the research underlying the Developmental Assets framework—not only to find out about assets in general, but more specifically to determine what needed to be done with the young people in the community. They created Link Crew (compare with Mark Hendrix's Link Crew in Garden Valley, California), says Piper, due to the disheartening information they received from Search Institute's *Profiles of Student Life: Attitudes and Behaviors* survey:

> *The students chose to solve the schoolwide absence of assets by creating their mentoring program for the underclassmen. YEP strongly believed that students would gain greater self-worth and brighter futures, and in turn create a community that values their youth. All hours of the day, Karrie Docterman worked side by side with her students, developing their skills as asset builders and sending them into the community willing and waiting to help those they encountered.*

Link Crew is currently 100 students, 28 of whom are in Karrie's class and act as mentors for younger students. Every grade 9 student in Rogers

High School is paired with a junior or senior as a mentor. These mentors are also mentored—by students from nearby Gonzaga University.

In the Link class, Karrie explains what the 40 assets are and gives students checklists to see which assets they report having. Then she, along with the students, develops activities to meet the needs expressed on the checklists. For example, students reported having a problem with time management, so she worked with them on setting goals. The students themselves suggested passing along what she taught them— say, avoiding peer pressure, or discussing competition and cooperation—to first-year students. As Shaina, a current student, describes:

> *[Karrie] put the whole thing together and made sure it ran smoothly all year, organizing activities and events, sorting link alerts that came in, and made connections with community members for mentorships as well. She does so much—not to mention that she is the ASB adviser and runs the whole leadership program at school on top of that. She was the Youth Empowerment adviser last year also and did an outstanding job with keeping us on track and focused. She does all these things to better her students' lives, and she should be recognized greatly for the extraordinary work that she has the drive to do. She is definitely my mentor, and I look up to her every day.*

Besides coordinating the Link Crew, Karrie teaches two classes of advanced placement U.S. history (for juniors), honors world history (for sophomores), advisory twice a week for study skills, American studies (for juniors), and leadership (for class officers). She participates in other activities as well, such as a volleyball rally every other month.

And over the summer she created Goals Organization Leadership and Development (GOLD), an asset-based program that includes such activities as how students can communicate better with their parents and how they can become more involved in their community. All students except those at academic risk receive the program now.

The establishment of GOLD in and of itself speaks to Karrie's ability to transform the norm, to cause a shift in the attitudes of people in the school community so that building assets is an expectation, not an exception. The more sources from which students can get those messages of strength—"You can do this." "You matter." "You're valuable."—the more likely they'll internalize them. The more connections are made throughout the school, the more momentum will be created.

As Wallace Williams, principal of Rogers High School, points out, most adult leaders in school become leaders through traditional roles, such as coach, but Karrie created her own leadership role. "She has a real clear passion for working with young kids, and that passion drives her to look at them as individuals," he says. "She creates an environment that students are proud of. . . . She makes things happen. Kids watch that, get inspired, and try to emulate her."

Karrie believes that most of the important, inspiring experiences for students happen outside the classroom. She has students over to her house, for study sessions and barbecues, so they can see her as a "real person," as approachable. Every good teacher Karrie remembers did something outside the classroom—attended her games, pushed her to do things. "I can't imagine being *just* a teacher," she says.

Still, she's cutting back. She has a five-year-old who's now starting school, so she looks for where other people can pick up her duties. "Sometimes I think that I'm the only one who can do things," says Karrie. Now, however, "I've really realized that letting students make mistakes is okay. The failures will make them stronger. I can't always make them perfect. Giving them more ownership is good for me."

Dani, currently a freshman at Washington State University, had Karrie for the leadership class, Link Crew, and advanced placement U.S. history. She can't begin to list all the ways that Karrie helped her. Shy and initially totally intimidated by Karrie, she'd heard that Karrie was a "tough teacher with very high expectations." By the end of her high school experience, however, Dani was making presentations—along with others—to the Spokane City Council, city department heads, the school board, and the mayor. As Dani says, "There's more of a sense that I can accomplish things now, because we did so much." Karrie is so successful, adds Dani, because "she has such a passion for what she does."

That passion rings out in Emily's testimonial for Karrie. Emily was part of YEP for two years:

She was always there telling us that we can make a difference and that our opinion and voice mattered. I remember countless times of going into that class and not thinking that what we were doing mattered, but Ms. Docterman always reminded us to not give up and that what we were doing was important.

One thing that I love about her is that even though she has all of these things going on in her life, she always makes sure everyone around her is doing okay. I remember in class, if there was someone that was looking down or sad, she was always there to see how they were doing or to see if she could help them in any way. She truly shows selflessness and true caring toward everyone. . . .

I know that all of these attributes of her character have had an impact on me. I remember at the end of my junior year, I had run for ASB president and had lost, and I was thinking of going off to Running Start for college my senior year and leave everything I had done behind at high school. I remember Ms. Docterman coming to me and saying that she wanted me to stay because she needed me to be in her leadership class, and that I would be missing out on everything if I went to college [early]. I am so grateful that she said that to me. My last year of high school was by the far the best year that I have had in my life. It was because of her genuine and sincere concern for me that I was able to have that amazing year. And it's just not me whom she has helped. There have been countless others.

One of the countless others was a recent student of Karrie's. His mom sent him to Spokane from California to live with his older sister, because he was involved with gangs, his brother was a heavy drug dealer, and he had a history of child assault—as both victim and perpetrator.

"He was a pretty rough kid when he came here," Karrie says. He was very quiet, and she talked to him all the time. Eventually, he got involved in sports and other activities; he found an outlet for his energy and his talents. By his senior year, he was able to make a presentation at a family breakfast and talk about how he'd changed, particularly because of the positive adults in his life. He graduated two years ago. He currently attends Whitworth College and wants to be a counselor.

Lisa Mattson, who's the coordinator of SHAPES (Spokane High Achieving and Performing Schools) and has worked closely with Karrie, says she's somewhat in awe of her: "She is just driven. She seeks excellence in every aspect of her life. Pair that with her passion for kids in our community, [and] everything feels possible."

Lisa remembers when Karrie empowered her students to identify community resources for young people. Her students surveyed 400 adults as well as every business in the local Yellow Pages. They compiled all the information, made recommendations and presentations—they took over the project. Two of those students eventually traveled with Lisa to Atlanta to represent Spokane in competing for the "All-America City" award, which recognizes civic excellence and successful resolution of critical community issues. They won—the first time Spokane has had that distinction in 30 years.

"You would look at them," says Lisa, "and think they were run-of-the-mill, ordinary kids." But, she explains, Karrie's belief in them made them leaders—polished and worldly, when in fact they'd never traveled at all. "She builds the environment," says Lisa, "for students to build assets every day."

Sometimes, Karrie admits, she has taken a leadership role out of guilt because no one else will. It's the students who really inspire her: "I want kids to feel that they can empower themselves to make decisions . . . to think for themselves. . . . Academics is not what's going to make them a successful person. The more assets they have, the more successful they'll be in life. . . . When you get the thank-you notes or they're so sad because they have to leave school—that's when you say, 'Oh, *that's* why I do what I do.'"

> > >

hardworking teachers build connections throughout the community. People have likened Developmental Assets to a movement, and you can see that most clearly when an entire community adopts the asset framework. Teachers are in great positions to take the lead in this effort—first, because they know their students so well; second, because they know their students' parents; and third, because they're able to reach out to so many sectors of the community as an extension of their curricula. Think of the synergy when young people can get help building assets from the owner of the gas station on the corner, from the local PTA, from the manager of the local television station, from the home for the elderly, from the college football team, and from the mayor's office. You can start building these connections, and you'll be amazed at how others will keep the effort alive.

kim rampmeyer

> PRESCHOOL–GRADE 6
> WILLARD L. BOWMAN ELEMENTARY SCHOOL, ANCHORAGE, AK

It was a beautiful day in greater Anchorage, and Darrell Vincek, principal of Willard L. Bowman Elementary School, had taken his children on a bike ride. Along the way, they met up with a few other Bowman families.

Soon they stopped at a rest area, where the young students took an interest in an art display that featured different surfaces of gravel and other materials. Darrell observed the students setting up a scenario in which the ground was composed of lava and safe areas.

And then a marvelous thing happened: Rather than racing to see who could make it across the lava first, the students worked cooperatively to help each other get across. Darrell knew immediately that these students had been taught the spirit of cooperation by an exceptional physical education teacher—Kim Rampmeyer.

Kim teaches 42 (42!) 30-minute classes every week to more than

500 students, all of whom she knows by name. To ensure making a connection right from the start of the school year, Kim spends the month of August taking time to look over the prior year's yearbook to review the names and faces of students. "I know how important it is on those first few days of school to feel as if they belong," she says, "that someone knows who they are and remembers them."

Every day, every week, when students arrive at her class, they see simple door notes telling them what activities to do for the first few minutes of class. Often, they find partners. That gives Kim time to greet new students, work on behavior contracts, or talk with a teacher about any particular student.

In addition to teaching, Kim participates in a variety of community events. There's the "Heart Run," of course. And there's the "Fall Carnival." And then there's "Family Math and Science Night," "City-Wide Clean-up," "Hoop Shoot," and "Jump Rope for Heart."

Let's not forget the "Induction" program, an orientation for incoming staff developed by Kim and a colleague. The orientation includes a handbook, meetings, e-mail messages, and continual support throughout the year. The entire school district has now adopted this program.

Kim's also active in the PTA, the National Association for Sports and Physical Education, and both the Alaska and the northwest district of the American Alliance for Health, Physical Education, Recreation, and Dance. Just as important, she performs duties as a crossing guard, for which she often dons a *Cat in the Hat* hat.

Although Kim has a minor in math, she never really thought about teaching anything other than physical education. Sometimes it's frustrating: She's had students who have been heavy and yet she looks at their lunches and they're eating junk. Their parents don't support them or follow through with what she's doing. Kim realizes that she can't do much about the situation at that age; her students don't choose what they eat. So she works on the self-esteem part of it, encouraging all her students to feel good about their strengths—by building Developmental Assets.

And she builds Developmental Assets wherever she can. She plays "Compliment Tag" with her younger students to reinforce vocabulary.

Students are frozen by someone saying something negative to them, but can be released back into the game by someone laying their hand on the frozen student's shoulder, looking them in the eye, saying their name, and giving them a compliment.

She also plays a game called "Shape Museum," in which students form themselves into interesting shapes and become statues. Kim dusts the shapes with a "magic" cloth, so when she turns on music and turns off the lights, the dusted shapes become alive. The students dance or skip around quietly, find a statue to copy, and take on their form, thus releasing that statue to now dance or skip around the museum.

Within the three-minute song, the students will get to copy and be copied 8 to 10 times. Kim says, "I've learned that students feel validated when they are copied; it allows them to connect with others whom they usually don't interact with; it may open some communication or interactions between genders, nationalities, et cetera; students watch classmates and appreciate their abilities."

Sometimes the results of making such connections can be pretty dramatic, as Kim relates:

> I have a sixth-grade girl [Michelle], who told me she wasn't in band anymore and would like to come and help me three times per week when the rest of her class attends band. I agreed. The girl is very quiet, a little overweight, wears very baggy clothes to hide her body, works hard in P.E. class, and works at blending in wherever she can. When she comes to help, I try to have small tasks for her to do, prepping equipment for me, taking down or putting up bulletin boards, and so on. Two of the three days she is with me, I ask her to help me with a challenging kindergarten class. She is quick to jump in and go to those students who need extra attention or direction.

Kim's philosophy is to use every bit of her classroom, school, and community to help students feel successful. She wants them to feel safe enough "to try new and challenging activities without fear of teasing, bullying, failure, or rejection." The assets work perfectly into this philosophy, and Kim advises, "Don't struggle over it. Look at one or two of those 40 and try to work on a couple of them at a time."

It's a good guideline. If you sincerely want to build Developmental Assets in your classroom and in your school, don't expect to focus on all 40 every day. The more you can seamlessly—but intentionally— work the assets into your curriculum, the more natural it will seem for both you and your students. Safety, Positive Peer Influence, Responsibility, and Interpersonal Competence are all good bets to weave into P.E. The more able you are to do such weaving, the easier you'll find it to incorporate the asset framework into everything you do. The "hard work" may happen more in the planning stage than at any other time.

And hard work or not, the wonderful feedback from students is immeasurable. Here are just a few praises from some of Kim's students:

Thank you for helping me reach my goals for this quarter. Now I can make more goals for next quarter and I hope you help me with them, too.

JORDIN, GRADE 3

I would like to thank you for getting us stronger every day, for caring when we are hurt, and for making our day happy when we are having a bad day.

AMBERLY, GRADE 4

When I grow up I want to be just like you! You are my role model. I really owe you one.

ALEXIS, GRADE 5

I appreciate you because you have helped me a lot in gym. I was out of shape and lazy before I started coming to school, but now, since you have made us exercise, now I am back in shape.

EVAN, GRADE 6

The parents of Kim's students have their own stories to tell. Says Richard, whose fourth-grade daughter, Nicole, has had Kim for a teacher since kindergarten:

Last spring, my daughter was apprehensive at the prospect of rollerblading in P.E. class. On the first day of skating, when I picked her up after school, I asked how it had gone. "Mrs. Rampmeyer is the best P.E. teacher in the world!" she blurted out, launching into an account of how Mrs. Rampmeyer had begun by teaching the kids about safety equipment and "how to fall without getting hurt." Then, the more skilled skaters helped the beginners take their first steps. My daughter was so pleased by her success at rollerblading that we immediately drove to a store to buy a pair of skates.

Nicole puts it into her own 10-year-old language: "She's very friendly. Sometimes she talks to you first, and that encourages you to talk."

And what does Kim get out of all this? On the one hand, it's very simple to her: "I get to play with the kids." But on another level, it's so much more than that—it's about making a difference not only for the here and now with a particular student, but for the long run, for the community. Just take Michelle: All Kim's hard work made a huge impact. As Kim tells the story:

About a month ago, [Michelle's] class went on a field trip and she was not able to go. She and another student came and helped me for most of the day. During my planning time, we were all working in the equipment room and the two of them were talking. Michelle told me that she had decided that she now wants to become a P.E. teacher since working with me. She said she's always liked physical activity, but didn't realize how rewarding it can be to help others become successful. I felt this was a big revelation, especially for someone who is not what I would call athletic or with a stereotypical athletic build. She told me she hadn't really wanted to go on to college, but was now thinking it would be worth it if she could help kids.

teachers unite!

this book profiles trusting, engaging, asset-building, caring, hard-working teachers. You've met 18 of these teachers, every one of them helping to build Developmental Assets and making positive impacts on the students they come into contact with. I hope they've inspired you to do likewise.

Most of these teachers *have* been supported by administrators, colleagues, parents, and, of course, students. And in many of these cases, the support has been critical. It's the principals who allow classes on leadership to be taught in the first place. It's the colleagues who cofacilitate discussion groups. It's the parents who report on how much their children have thrived with their newfound roles. And it's the students who succeed at levels they never before imagined.

Some of these teachers, however, have fought continual battles to incorporate the Developmental Assets framework into their schools—battles against administrators, against colleagues, against parents, and students, too. Some of these teachers are lonely warriors indeed, and the fact that they've persevered in what some consider to be unorthodox pedagogy (letting students take responsibility) is yet another source of inspiration.

All teachers have a potential for building relationships with students, says Gary Mazzola, an asset champion and principal of Parkway South High School in Manchester, Missouri, where both Andie Brown and Martha Roper teach. What's more, he hires teachers based in part on their ability to have those relationships. As he says, "Who do you do your best work for? Those whom you like? Or those whom you're afraid of? Challenges and expectations are better motivators than rules and regulations." It's this kind of leadership that is essential to supporting great teachers and making schools rich with Developmental Assets.

Reading these profiles, you may have been struck by the praise heaped upon the teachers by their colleagues. That praise is more than merely a recognition of good work. These are strong feelings of camaraderie, of *partnership* in these schools. When teachers enlist their colleagues to adopt the asset framework, they find that they have a common language, common strategies, and common goals to interact with one another and all students in the school, not just in their own classroom. It feels good to be part of a team with an honorable mission.

These teachers have also involved students' families in their asset-building efforts. They've sent home asset checklists for families to discuss. They've brought families into the school to show them how their children have achieved. And, above all, they've communicated. They've become familiar with their students' families as a way to better understand their students. And they've found valuable allies in those families.

You've read about relationships between students and teachers throughout this book. Those relationships are absolutely essential to building assets—for two reasons. One reason is that if you as a teacher are going to be able to influence your students, you're going to have to trust in them and engage them with your caring. You're going to have to understand who they uniquely are.

The other reason is that once you've got their attention, you can help them along the way to building assets. Students need help. They need you to be there to support them, to empower them, to set boundaries and expectations, to show them how to use their time constructively, to encourage their commitment to learning, to model positive values, to teach them social competencies, and to guide them toward forging a positive identity.

You don't have to go it alone to help build Developmental Assets. You'll be more successful when you bring aboard the entire school and the greater community.

Think about this in terms of violence prevention. You can show students in your class how violence is hurtful. You can teach those students skills to avoid violent situations. But when your students venture out into the hallway or the playground or the parties, and their peers have neither the skills nor the motivation to use those skills, they may be in trouble, regardless of your efforts. It's when students get consistent nonviolence messages from other teachers, from members of their family, and from their friends that the norm in the school community begins to solidify against violence.

It's the same with Developmental Assets. You can be a port in a storm, in which students receive warmth and approbation and respect when they're not being battered everyplace else. But how much more powerful it would be if there were several ports: other classrooms, the school bus, a friend's house. Home.

Take care of yourself first. But don't discount the support of others.

firing up and burning out

Continuing to be hardworking and not burn out in teaching requires ongoing strategizing and evaluating choices. One issue all teachers face daily that can greatly affect their ability to be trusting, engaging, asset building, caring, and hardworking is that of *boundaries*.

Some teachers want to be involved with their students continually, whether it's answering their phone calls any time of the day or night, chaperoning them on weekend trips, inviting them into their homes, or visiting with their families. These teachers recognize a need in their students that can be met only by their utter devotion, and in fact they enjoy and take energy from that devotion.

Other teachers *want* some respite from their professional duties but find it difficult to separate. And a few teachers in this book deliberately and effectively "leave the school behind" when they go home.

Along with these geographical and programmatic boundaries exist emotional boundaries. All of these teachers, no matter how fired up they are about their students' successes, have to exercise care that they don't burn out at their failures. For however many students they teach who go on to college, open a profitable business, or form a beautiful family, there are also those students who drop out of school, get strung out on drugs, or fall in with the wrong crowd. For all the successful students whom these teachers are able to steer on a healthy, productive path, there's inevitably another student who veers from that path despite their best efforts. Yet all the teachers profiled in this book have found strategies to address those failures and to keep teaching with vigor and hope.

One of these strategies is the "Individual Responsibility" strategy. It goes like this:

> *I have given this student my time, my energy, my knowledge, and my compassion. I have sought out a myriad of ways to make a connection. I have faithfully tried to build assets by establishing a respectful relationship, providing a supportive environment, and implementing programs and practices that give this student an opportunity to thrive. I've done all I can with this student. But at some point this student has to take some responsibility.*

The second strategy is the "Never Give Up" strategy, and it goes like this:

> *I can't seem to get through to this student, but I'm going to keep trying. There must be something I haven't thought of—some interest, some family member, some learning style, some strength that I haven't tapped. I need to ask this student more questions, talk with more people who know this student, and continue to brainstorm methods of building this student's assets. I just know I can be effective if only I can figure out the key to unlock this student's resistance.*

And a third strategy is the "Johnny Appleseed" strategy:

> *I've given it my best, and I'm not sure whether I've made any headway. But somewhere down the road, the seeds I've sown may sprout. Weeks, months, years from now, this student may be in a situation and remember something I said, something I did. Then the strength will be acknowledged, the asset come to fruition, the insight used for good. Neither this student nor I have any way of knowing when that will happen, but I have to have confidence that it indeed will happen.*

Regardless of the grade you teach, there may be failures. And just as the successes are likely to elate, the failures may frustrate. How you approach each is key.

The effectiveness of these strategies depends on the individual. Use what works best for you. Remember, though: There are numerous stories of students returning to teachers years later, saying, in effect, "Thank you for what you did." In some of these cases, the teacher barely remembers the student. That's why—to return to the Johnny Appleseed strategy—you have to carry a lot of seeds with you and spread them far and wide.

Great teachers do that.

great teachers

These are the teachers profiled in this book:

peggy allen

South Lebanon Elementary School
50 Ridgeview Lane
South Lebanon, OH 45039

andrea (andie) godfrey brown

Parkway South High School
801 Hanna Road
Manchester, MO 63021

susan cressey

Kennebunk High School
89 Fletcher Street
Kennebunk, ME 04043

karrie docterman

Rogers High School
1622 East Wellesley Avenue
Spokane, WA 99207

susie edwards

DeMille Elementary School
5400 Van Buren Street
Midway City, CA 92655

sandy eggleston

Pine Brook Elementary School
2300 English Road
Rochester, NY 14616

melinda (mindy) ellerbee

Williams Elementary School
507 East University Drive
Georgetown, TX 78626

jenny goldberg-mc donnell

Kepner Middle School
911 South Hazel Court
Denver, CO 80219

beth grove

O'Neill Elementary School
24701 San Doval Lane
Mission Viejo, CA 92691

mark hendrix

Golden Sierra High School
5101 Garden Valley Road, P.O. Box 175
Garden Valley, CA 95633

tom kidd

DeLong Middle School
2000 Vine Street
Eau Claire, WI 54703

pam medzegian

South Salem High School
1910 Church Street South
Salem, OR 97302

kim rampmeyer

Willard L. Bowman Elementary School
11700 Gregory Road
Anchorage, AK 99516

martha roper

Parkway South High School
801 Hanna Road
Manchester, MO 63021

kathi swanson

Lower Macungie Middle School
6299 Lower Macungie Road
Macungie, PA 18062

sue walker

Warren Township High School
34090 Almond Road
Gurnee, IL 60031

michael walsh

Ursa Major Elementary School
164 Dyea Street
Fort Richardson, AK 99505

sean yeager

South Middle School
229 West Greenhurst Road
Nampa, ID 83686

acknowledgments

What a treat to be able to interview such outstanding teachers. I thank each and every one of them: They hosted me in their schools, they talked with me about their professional and personal lives, they gave me samples of their students' work, and they referred me to other people who know their work. I thank all the administrators, colleagues, parents, community workers, and, of course, students who contributed their observations.

I thank Ruth Taswell, Marcie Rouman, and Kay Hong, my editors at Search Institute, for their suggestions and management of the book. I also thank the reviewers whose feedback improved the text.

Finally, I thank the principals whose stewardship provides an environment in which these teachers can thrive. Some principals, to be sure, are more supportive than others; but to those who recognize what gems they have in their schools and act on that recognition, know that you are appreciated.